Better
Boating Blunders

Seagoing Stuff-Ups
for
Beginners and Experts

Paul Curtis

Illustrated by
John Quirk

Other Books by Paul Curtis:
High Tea on the Cunard Queens
Aboard Pacific Princess
The Oasis Sisters
History of Professional Photography in Australia

Other Books by John Quirk
Foul Bottoms

 Rose Publishing
www.rosepublishing.com.au

First Published 2021

© Paul Curtis 2021

The right of Paul Curtis to be identified as The Author has been asserted in accordance with the Copyright, Design and Patents Act 1988.

Illustrations: Copyright: ©John Quirk 2021

All rights reserved. No part of this book may be reprinted or reproduced or utilised in any form or by electronic, mechanical or other means now known or hereafter invented, including photocopying or recording, or in any information and storage or retrieval system without the permission in writing from the publishers.

ISBN: 978-0-6452487-0-8

*There are good ships
and wood ships,
Ships that sail the sea,
But the best ships
Are friendships,
May that always be.*

　　　　　　　　-Irish Proverb

CONTENTS

ONE	Negotiating Your Boat: Do's and Don'ts	6
TWO	Build Your Own: The Hull Truth	28
THREE	What's in a Name: Choosing Something Sweet	42
FOUR	Anchors Aweigh: Amusing the Onlooker	52
FIVE	Navigation and Pilotage	76
SIX	Safe Communication: Is 'Over' Over?	88
SEVEN	Living Aboard While Saving Relationships	98
EIGHT	Keeping a Tender Behind	132
NINE	Maintaining Your Boat	154
TEN	Selling Your Boat	164
ELEVEN	Talking the Lingo	174

Negotiating Your Boat

Do's and Don'ts

ONE

Did you know some people don't like chocolate? Amazing, isn't it? But I read it in a newspaper, so it must be true. There seems no end to the little foibles and dislikes people come up with. I even heard of a chap, who on his introductory sail, went out on a friend's boat, came back, and said he didn't like boating. Imagine that.

This man was guilty of having condemned the whole concept based on one day out. The sea, the beaches, the gentle slap of waves on the hull as you explore new places: these are what boating is all about. And as that wise old Walrus so famously said, '...there is nothing, absolutely nothing, half so much worth doing as simply messing about in boats.'

Our misled friend was confused. So therefore, Doctor Phil, it was not the boating the man didn't like. It was the actual boat. QED. What he should have done, is buy his own boat.

There is a boat for all seasons. Whether you are pondering gliding silently under sail or have that dark need to noisily rip seas apart with a tidal-wave-inducing motor cruiser, you must take one essential step: consult your partner.

You will probably get the short, pithy answer 'Don't.' But be like the 97.9 percent of people we did not survey for this book and go ahead and buy one anyway. Remember, the key thing about statistics is that 68.2 percent of them are made up on the spot. You know you were going to do it, and after all, you're the boss around here. Aren't you?

The only reason for going through this vital consultation is to give off an aura of level headedness, indeed wisdom, plus a *soupçon* of nautical expertise. Handled carefully, it also imparts a sense of complicity in the decision-making process. Proudly announce to any audience of friends and relatives, that 'We've' decided to buy a boat, it will be fun for family and friends.' And who would dare argue with that? Oh, the power of the royal 'We'. Think of it as an exercise in covering your transom.

Don't listen to that nonsense about the word BOAT being an acronym for Bring on Another Thousand; give a dismissive chuckle when bores tell you a boat is a hole in the water into which you just pour money, give a superior smile when the racing yachty moans sailing is like standing under a cold shower while ripping up hundred-dollar bills. Be strong, give a knowing nod and a blind eye when passing that motorboat called *Ka-Ching*. You know better than these negative minded landlubbers because you know boating is 'Fun' and that now is the time for you to roll the dice and buy that boat.

It's off to the boat brokers we go. Let's leave the private sellers for a moment as here are dangerous shoals to be navigated. To avoid being left high and dry, great caution is needed. Professional brokers, for the main, are a good and happy lot who know all the ropes. But a few might use this skill to tie you up in knots.

Before you cross their bows for the first time, even up the odds a bit and be sure you're buying yourself the right type of boat. The first questions a broker is likely to ask is where do you want to go, how do you want to get there, what you want to do when you get there and how many passengers are you likely to carry? Being unable to answer any of these will, for the wrong sort of broker, tattoo sucker bait right across your forehead. Now we don't want that, do we?

There's a multitude of different types of boats to choose from. Whereas McDonalds ask, 'Would you like fries with that?' we ask ourselves would we like a mast with that? Just one, or fancy maybe two, or go the whole hog and have three?

Those who don't want any masts at all can skip the next few paragraphs and go straight to the good oil on motor and rowboats. If you want to save the cost of one oar, go for a canoe.

Back to masts. In a nutshell: three masts mean you're opting for a schooner, which is okay. It could also be a clipper, a brig, a brigantine, or a barquentine. These are not okay. Doesn't matter which of these rigs you go for, it is a waste of money. You'll be spending a fortune on sails and rigging and will need a football team to come sail with you.

Yes, I am sure there are some advantages to clippers, brigs and brigantines, but at the moment it is hard to think of any: unless you fancy climbing masses of rigging and loudly calling "Land Ho!" to an assembled crew below.

For trading vessels, they have the advantage of more hold space, but as sailing trading vessels sailed off into the sunset a hundred years ago, it is hard to figure why people are still making them? However, for a sail training boat for young adventurers, it is a reasonable excuse.

Settle on only two masts and you have a variety of options. Put the small mast up at the front and you will have a sensible, manageable schooner. Not to be confused with an Australian beer glass, a schooner does look a bit back to front and at first glance, people might think you're sailing backwards.

Put the shorter mast at the back and call it a mizzen and you will have a ketch. Move the mizzen a bit further back, in an afterthought position behind the rudder post, and you will have a yawl. For a yawl, your nautical attire is important. To play the part properly, it is compulsory to wear a Greek fisherman's hat, a blue and white striped jersey, and be puffing on a curly briar pipe. You will look the real deal. Or maybe a bit of a twat.

In any beauty parade, the ketch or the yawl are the most curvaceous, hottest, downright sexiest looking boats in the parade. Two masts are better than one you know. They steer themselves under sail and at anchor the mizzen boom is an ideal place to hang your washing. In a rolling anchorage, leave the mizzen sail up and sheeted in tight and you will have a wonderful flopper stopper, leaving you sitting calmly while others will be rolling their insides out. On a ketch, no gin will be spilt, and you'll sleep like a baby. Bliss.

If the mizzen is missing and you have only one mast, then it is generally called a sloop. This one mast option is the most popular and is often bought by people who don't have enough money for two. It is also fashionable with the racing fraternity, god bless 'em, as they have a perverted and ungentlemanly desire to beat close to windward. Cruising types find them easier to handle which is just as well as they seem to have less friends.

Racing types seem to need at least a dozen fully testosterone-charged mates. Mostly rigged Bermudan style, with one sail at the front and another at the back, it needs less rigging and sails, thus giving a clearer sunbathing space on deck. Important that.

Sloop *Yawl* *Ketch*

An unpredictably swinging boom, conveniently located at head height, helps stretch out the mainsail. It can also cause a bit of a headache. To avoid this worry, some, generally in the older age bracket, take to rigging their boom at the top of the mast. Now called a gaff rather than a boom, it is less troublesome way up there, but heaven help you if its halyard rope breaks and the spar comes crashing down. But that, I guess, is all part of the fun of sailing. Hey, we never said it was going to be easy.

So, with the top bits of sailing boats now sorted, let's get down to the hull. Again, do you want one, two, or three? Anyone that wants more than three, please leave now.

A mono hull glides beautifully through the water and is easier and generally cheaper to find somewhere to keep, whether on a mooring or in a marina berth. But, under way, sailing sloops tend to develop a bit of a lean to one side. This can either be exhilarating or scare you to death. The choice is yours. Mind you, depending on the sea conditions, moving about the boat is a tad more difficult. There is no doubt that mobility is slightly impaired, although it does help if you have one leg longer than the other.

How Many Hulls?

Get two hulls joined at the naval and you have a cat. This Siamese arrangement is no pussy, it's a catamaran. They are fast sailing off the wind, but not so good into it. They draw little water, so you can get in nice and close to the beach and thus only have a short row to shore in the dingy. But enter a marina, and you can expect to pay double. However, at sea your boat will stay nice and level. This makes it a particular favourite for those of us who enjoy a quiet tipple while under way as the beer does not slide off the cockpit table.

The two hulls tend to be narrow and thus have less room for double beds. In smaller catamarans, this often leads to one partner sleeping in one hull and the other partner in the hull next door. This is either good or bad for your relationship. Only you can work that out. And good luck with that.

Not that either party is likely to get much sleep. The noise of the water slapping and echoing between the hulls would drown out a Rolling Stones concert.

Three hulls? Then you have a trimaran. What were you thinking? You have not only increased the advantages over a catamaran by one third, but you have done the same to the disadvantages. Where are you going to moor her? However, they are good for threesomes. Anything more than three hulls is deemed excessive.

By now you may have decided to simplify the whole box and dice. Do you really need a sailing boat with a boom to bang your head, a raised steel cleat to stub a wayward bare toe, and wire shrouds garrotting your neck? Chuck the whole bleeding lot over the side and you get: ta-da: a motorboat.

Okay, you pedants out there, we know it could also be a rowing boat. But if that's all you're interested in, leave us alone and stick to your ponds.

Also suited only for ponds is the coracle. Completely round shaped, it was used by early man with just one paddle, thus mostly going around and around with little forward movement. Its only possible use would be for circumnavigations. For the rest of us, the only need for a proper rowing boat is for getting us ashore to the nearest pub.

Motorboats, commonly called stink boats by the sailing fraternity, also come in a wide variety of sizes and types. You must choose between stately chug-chugging along at trotting speed in a displacement boat or go for a fuel-guzzling screamer that half-leaps out of the water and roars off with a thunderclap, quickly vanishing behind its own mountainous wake.

If choosing the latter, the screaming will mainly come from your bank manager, as your fuel bill rapidly chews through your life savings. Moving at a stately trot will be both peaceful and more economic, but don't expect to be first back to the yacht club bar.

Now we come to the issue of power: one engine or two. Are two engines twice as good as one? Well, if you're worried about engine failure in the middle of the ocean, it does double your chances of getting home. It also doubles your annual maintenance bills. Inboard engines make for a classier look but make for noisier installations and difficulty of engine service access. Outboard engines are now becoming the rage on small to medium boats as you gain boat room and servicing is cheaper. But the looks!

If you're thinking of an inboard petrol engine, don't. You don't want to be sitting on a tank of gallons of petrol. Unless you don't mind the idea of one day being possibly flambéed for breakfast.

Choosing a Bottom

Finishing off our list of things to know before buying, don't forget to sneak a peek under the waterline. This part of the boat you only hope to see on a slipway is the underwater part of the hull. It is affectionately known as 'the bottom'. You should become an expert in these. A nicely rounded one will glide easily through the water, but all those curves will tend to slow you down. If you put a bit of flair along the waterline with a sharp bend, it is called a hard chine. Given enough power from either engine or wind, the boat first rears her bow and then settles down to a fast pace, skimming along on her chines. We are now planing. It's exhilarating and lots of fun.

While we're down here, sailing types should take a good look at the keel. A short deep keel is much favoured by racing yachties. Not only does it generate less water drag than a full-length keel, but it gives their skippers a look of extreme professionalism when backing into marinas. A full-length keel is more seaworthy, better for crossing bars at the river mouth and generally protects the propeller from being the first thing to hit the rocks. While the insurance company will be happy, backing this type of boat is a bit tricky as it takes around three boat lengths to get any kind of steerage way.

Armed, with this vast imparted knowledge and now knowing exactly what we are looking for, we are ready to approach the boat broker.

If you are buying new, don't spend too long gloating over the brochure. Just wipe your drool away and get ready for your first real look. Ha! See, those photos were the fraudulent work of a special wide-angle lens beloved by house and boat sellers. That wide-open companionway looking like a six-lane highway in the photos will take a month of dieting to squeeze through; while that roomy, airy saloon is best navigated by a bulimic fashion model. For this reason, when inspecting a boat, take plenty of your own pics. They will give some slight vestige of reality.

Now for the price, proudly displayed on a piece of paper which, for some reason, is generally separate from the brochure. But there it is in black and white. One might think buying new means there is no room for negotiation. There's the list price and that's that. But that slip of paper tucked into the brochure is easily reprinted.

It's just a little litmus test to assess the extent of your green and readies. It is there to check your defences: the opening salvo for the long battle ahead while keeping firm reins on your desires: men dream of bikini clad beauties on the foredeck; ladies dream of pina coladas and men doing the cooking and washing up.

Let the buyer versus vendor match begin. The bell has been rung for the first arduous bout. In one corner, we have our lovesick, boat-buying dreamer. In the other corner, we have our smooth and amenable broker: confident, knowledgeable, worldly and with order book eagerly clenched in hand.

Am I being a bit harsh on the noble art of boat broking? Well, it's called broking for a reason: when you finish, you'll be broke. The broker may well be a good, decent type, adviser, and potential friend. They will certainly be that when it's time to sell your boat. But for now, they are your adversary. Settle in for a long beat to windward.

Seamanship shouldn't be confused with salesmanship. Start off by carefully studying the list of inclusions. Have essential items been omitted? Is the gear up to spec?

Some brokers have been known to confuse the price by adding free add-ons, such as throwing in an anchor, but no chain. The excuse is 'I didn't know if you wanted rope or chain.' Then you must check the anchor is man enough and not something a good seaman would sneer at as only suitable for a paperweight. Take nothing for granted, or nothing is what you will get.

For instance, I once had a broker who on a new boat tried to make like a hero by offering to throw in free antifouling on a large sailing boat. Generous that. I was underwhelmed. And, if you're buying one of those wretched large motor cruiser things, (must you?) check to see how much fuel will be in the tanks when it is delivered. Right there, you can save a few thousand.

Wheeling and Dealing

The successful boat buyer must be a skilful negotiator. Negotiating is a dark and mysterious art and for the best deal you need to be as adept as a one-armed trapeze skiff sailor preparing to hoist a spinnaker. You can buy whole books on the subject. Not on one armed skiff sailors, but on negotiating. You will be glad to know this isn't one of them. I have, however, read quite a few and I have been to numerous conferences in Las Vegas. So there. Thus, I am in the ideal position to share with you my bounteous knowledge.

Let me tell you what goes on in Las Vegas. It's about time someone did. It's a terrible place: very dry, lots of sand yet no beach to launch even a canoe. Nothing to do but go to conferences. Terrible. The place is always chock-a-block with conferences filled with motivational speakers telling you how to make your fortune. Needless to say, they mostly made their own by speaking at conferences and selling books about it rather than actually doing what the book is advocating. Huh? If they're so damned rich and successful, why are they at this cruddy convention?

Nevertheless, we get inspired, filled with enthusiasm and worst still, horror-horror, overflowing with new ideas. You are remodelled and can't wait to get back to the office and get stuck into changing things to a new order of business. When you stride purposefully back to work, chest inflated with new vim and vigour, your co-workers quickly dash into hiding. But they are not alarmed. They recognise this annual phenomenon and know you'll be back to your old ways by week's end.

Although I must confess to having enduring memories of a talk entitled *'You Can Negotiate Anything'*. It was delivered by the very charismatic and witty American called Herb Cohen, a former White House negotiator. He had already proved his skills by negotiating his speaker's fee. Not only did he share his secrets, but he also sold us his books.

He told a story of how he negotiated a hotel room in a full-up Washington when the whole city was booked out. At the desk, he first made out he had made a booking, when he hadn't. Naughty that. The desk clerk insisted they had not received a booking and the hotel didn't have any rooms left. So,

Herb called for the manager. A long discussion ensued. There were a few mutterings and rebellious groans from the long and weary check-in line behind. Herb was having no luck. After about ten minutes of argy-bargy, he finally said to the manager: 'If the President of the United Sates comes here tonight, you would find a room for him, wouldn't you?'

The manager conceded he would. Herb promptly pulled out his phone, punched some buttons, muttered a few words, hung up and said, 'I've just spoken to his people, and I can tell you he's not coming. I'll have his room.' And he got it!

Now you can see how very motivational and helpful it all was. At the end of his session, we leapt as one to our feet and applauded wildly. I turned to the man beside me and said, "Wasn't that wonderful?"

He nodded and dryly remarked the inspiration might last all the way back to the carpark.

One of Herb's golden rules is that in a negotiation you should care, but not too much. Sage advice well it might be, but when it comes to a new boat you have fallen heavily for, it's not so easy to follow. However, at least try to give the broker an illusion of nonchalance and not being particularly fussed about doing the deal. After all there are so many boats to choose from. Right?

I did buy Herb's book and I took away another tip that has stood me in good stead. And that is to endure and never give up. The trick is you drag out negotiations, so they go on and on…and on. Go over details endlessly, ask countless questions, make counter offers and the like for days, weeks, months. Blow first hot, then cold. When the broker feels he might be winning, play the cruel card that you are now considering another boat a bit cheaper.

Run the poor man through the whole gamut of human emotions: optimism, exhilaration, and despair. Wear the broker down to such an extent that he ends up having invested so much time negotiating, he is now more desperate for the sale than you are. At this stage, he is expertly persuading the boat's owner to just about agree to anything, if only to finally get rid of you. It's cruel, but it works.... mostly.

I tried this technique of protracted negotiation on the acquisition of my first cabin sailing boat, eighteen feet, hard-chined plywood sloop with the luxury of a bucket for the dunny. It was a New Zealand design called a Hartley Chuckles. There was not much to chuckle about. The cabin was tiny, only suitable for a friendless dwarf. But it was a cabin. A new luxury in a sailing boat for me.

The loo facility consisted of a plastic seat and steel frame propped over a clear plastic bag. After use, you added in a few stones, sealed the bag and simply dropped it over the side. Can you imagine that? No, best not to. It was decades ago in the environmentally unaware days of few boats and less people.

I first saw this new fancy of mine bobbing tantalising on a mooring directly in front of our island house. No, we were not living in a millionaire's waterfront mansion. Our home was little more than a timber boat shed. There was no reticulated water. We had to collect the rain off the roof into a rusty and leaky water tank. The dunny was out the back and shared with a menagerie of venomous snakes and spiders. With no road access, commuting to work was by getting into your dinghy and put-putting half a mile to the mainland. Then into our car and off we would go.

Sound romantic? Sometimes, but not always. Pouring cats and dogs in the middle of winter and dressed in a business suit, you first had to bail out your commuting dinghy. Weather gear, enabling you to perform this act without getting a stream of icy water right down your backbone, has yet to be invented.

Coveting Thy Neighbour's Aft

The voyage to the mainland always took us past this pretty little sailing boat and we could see all too well how sadly neglected she had become. The owner never came near and after a period of heavy rain, she would begin to fill and sink lower and lower.

She also had a long halo of seaweed around her topsides. Unable to bear the thought of her coming to a watery end, to the rescue I would go, wobbling along in my tiny dinghy to bail her out. See what a good fellow I am?

Financially, we were barely equipped to buy a toy boat for the bath. We were young, just married, had taken a huge home mortgage, and were amid a new business venture.

Ignoring the Eleventh Commandment, I nevertheless began to covet my neighbour's boat. I left a note on her asking the owner to contact me, but as he never came near, my message went unread. Setting about finding the name of the owner was no easy task. No freedom of information here. The harbour authority wouldn't tell, the local boatyards didn't know as, judging by the barnacles up to her waterline, she had never even glimpsed a slipway.

By dint of continually asking around, I finally managed to track down the owner. I rang, told him I liked his boat, and would he let me use her a bit as he didn't. He seemed a tad taken aback. But I explained that I would maintain and repair her, insure her and she would always be ready for his use whenever and if ever he chose to take her out.

He couldn't get over my cheek. He said he would like to think about it, probably for a decade or two. But I rang him again a few weeks later and told him his boat was once more riding perilously low. His boom cover was also flapping loose and would he mind awfully if I went over and fixed those problems. It was the middle of a cold and wet winter. He kindly let me.

Three such phone calls later, he finally agreed to meet and discuss my proposal. When we did, somewhat ruefully he agreed the deal, mainly, he claimed, as he had a good laugh out of it. He thought my negotiating style was akin to forgetting to duck when the skipper called 'lee-oh'.

He added, 'I guess I will never get around to going out in her, either with or without you.'

And he didn't. So, in effect, we had a free boat.

A Sad Ending

If I might track a bit off course for a moment, I must confess this boat had a very sad ending. She is the only boat I ever lost to a storm.

One dark night, with gale force winds and flooding rains on top of an exceptionally high tide, she broke her mooring and blew off unseen into the darkness.

After a couple of days, the weather cleared sufficiently for me to slap the outboard on the dinghy and go looking for her. After two miles of searching the lee shores, I finally found her. In front of a large and very stately home on the mainland was a seawater, rock swimming pool. And there, sticking out above the pool was her mast and bowsprit.

During the storm and floods, the bay's spring high tide had risen by around eight feet, and this is why she broke her mooring. At the storm's height, off she went and blew over the top of the pool's rock seawall. Trapped inside, she had beaten back and forth on the rocks until finally sinking to the bottom.

A short consultation with the homeowner, gave the impression that he was none too pleased to have an eighteen-foot, plywood cabin boat sunk at the bottom of his pool. My attempt at a merry ice-breaking quip that wasn't he a bit old to have a boat in his bath, did not seem to improve his disposition.

Marine surveyors, divers and insurance assessors were called. After consultations, it was decided to remove one side of the pool retaining wall, drag the boat out and then rebuild the swimming enclosure.

Our lovely little boat was deemed a total write-off. The insurance company was relatively happy to compensate us with the full insured sum. They were not so happy, however, to meet the costs of the salvage operation and the removal and replacement of the rock retaining walls. That worked out about fifteen times more expensive than the boat's value. Still, we now had the funds for another boat!

Hoist with Our Own Petard

A couple of decades and three boats later, the family fortunes had improved a bit and we fell for a very comfortable motor-sailer. It was just the thing for a family with young children and middle-aged parents. It had big windows to look out of and a comfortable armchair from which to do that looking. We were in love.

Unfortunately, the boat was advertised at a price twenty percent higher than we could afford. Our offer at this figure was sneered at by the broker. He said he wouldn't bother the owner with such a ridiculous offer. So, we again resorted to Mr Cohen's teachings.

We met the broker on board on five separate occasions. We looked under every seat cushion and carefully examined everything between the truck and the keel bolts. The poor old broker had all the gear out for us and then had to put it all back again. After three months of such visiting, we noticed a nervous tick developing in the broker's eye. We felt this was progress.

On the next visit the sail bags were dragged out and the sails pulled out for inspection. They were lovely and white and there was nere a sign of any daylight peeping through the seams. We checked the battens. Then we remembered another appointment and rushed off leaving the broker to bag them up again.

We talked of a slight increase in our offer and then made sure he was unable to reach us on the phone for a couple of weeks. We must have been a bit busy. When he finally got through, we told him we were very much attracted to a boat being handled by another broker. Hey, you've got to be a bit of a sadist in this game. You've got to make it an oar-deal, if you'll forgive the pun.

Thus challenged, the broker launched into full sales mode. The previous off-handedness was replaced with enthusiasm for doing a deal. He was now ready to put our new offer to the owner.

Unfortunately, the owner flat out rejected it, saying that he had his price and that was that. But, as the months went by, the boat remained on the market.

We then had a stroke of genius. Inflation was running high in those days and was hitting above fourteen percent. We did our sums and calculated that if he had accepted our offer, the owner would now have made up the difference in the price by just putting our money in a savings bank and earning the interest. Then we added on the vendor's cost of mooring, insuring, and maintaining the boat for those months and he was, in fact, financially way behind. He was losing money so fast it would be best for him to rush our deal through speedier than the after-boat race rush for the bar.

Yes! This was it. We had a winning case now.

Constraining our excitement, we called the broker and together we went through the figures. He checked and cross-checked, hand blurring as he punched his calculator. Yes, we were right! He would call his client right away. Rubbing our hands with glee, we waited on the answer. The owner asked for some time to check the figures.

Two days later, we got our answer. Yes, the owner agreed with our sums and thanked us for pointing it out. Accordingly, he decided to increase his asking price by twenty percent!

So, we never did get that boat. What's that? Serve us right you say.

Boat Shows

A boat show is a good place to hone your own negotiating skills. But beware of the situation where you are sitting comfortably in the cockpit, glass of champagne in one hand while the other is poised with pen quivering over a contract. Yes, I know it's a boat show special, but, just like furniture stores, there is always a sale on.

Negotiating at a show is just for practice. When you have a long line of potential buyers, even if some are fender kickers, waiting directly behind you, the salesman is in a blissful orgasmic state. We certainly don't want to negotiate with him in that condition. Wait a week until he is sitting lonely in his office and staring at a phone that just won't ring.

I'm very experienced at going to boat shows. I've been to them all ...some many times: London, Southampton, Miami, Newport, Sydney, Melbourne, Queensland Gold Coast, you name it. Ah yes, I know all about boat shows.

I know both sides of boat show deals as I once exhibited a new boat at a show myself. Observing the growing trend for grey nomads to get in their campervans and drive off on crowded roads all over the place, we noted these vans are more like mini apartments on wheels. So why shouldn't we build a boat like that? Surely, breezing along the coast would be far more fun than battling smelly, congestion choke points along a highway. To instead luxuriously cruise the open seas, would have retiring couples standing in long lines with cheque book eagerly clutched in hand.

We agreed to invest our life savings in the project. Well, I guess it was more my idea. I had to sleep in the spare room for a week. But we made some adaptions to a design for a fifty-two-foot pilot house motorboat that could be easily managed by an older couple.

We had her built by the Taiwanese in China and boy does she have everything: reclining armchairs, induction cooktops, automatic dishwasher and even a laundry washer and dryer. So manoeuvrable is she that docking in crowded marinas can be done easily and quietly: no fuss, no yelling, and no strain on matrimonial relations. Even landlubbers would die for this one.

The only problem was that it took two years to complete the project and when we finally received delivery, the world was plunged into the deepest darkness of history-making recession. There were not many visitors to the boat show that year. Even the market for paddleboards took a severe downturn. The only boat selling being done was by the banks. They had huge lists of repossessions.

These days I am back to boat show visiting as a buyer rather than a seller. In this capacity, I advise it is best to ignore the allure of all those Show-Only-Specials. The buy now prices so boldly proclaimed are a mere flash of vendor's fancy. Despite what you are told, they are certain to be available until next year's boat show. Then they will probably drop again. So, don't give in too soon.

Surveying

Negotiate like hell, then when you have finally arrived at the lowest price, call in the big guns. Before taking delivery, whether new, or pre-loved (ha-ha) call in your own surveyor. They can save you their fee many times over.

With the boat slipped, broker and owner nervously pacing about and your surveyor busily plunging his marlin spike into the boat's innermost, intimate entrails, it is a high anxiety time for everyone: it can set vendor, buyer and broker pacing about as if waiting for news outside a maternity unit.

There are basically two main types of surveyors: those that get most of their referrals from yacht brokers and those that manage the trickier process of establishing referrals from yacht buyers. These two groups tend to take different approaches to their craft.

The first are great mates with the brokers. Their surveys are more likely to temper any faults discovered as being consistent with the asking price. In pursuit of future referrals, some have been accused of even turning a blind eye to a few minor shortcomings.

The second group can be so keen to prove their worth to the buyer that they will take an excessively nit-picking approach.

There is a third group, which tends to take a more practical approach and be equally fair to both vendor and buyer. They do exist. You can find one.

I was talking to Ernie, our yacht club comedian who sits

at the corner of the bar waiting to trap the unwary. Ernie is a strict motorboat man and would have no truck with a sailing boat.

'Why on earth not?' I asked.

Ernie sniffs. Can't trust 'em, they're rigged.

Adds Ernie, 'I bet you don't even know the difference between a yacht and a boat.'

I shrug.

'About a million bucks'.

I can't stop him.

'What do you call a sail with only two corners?'

He answers his own question:

'I haven't got a clew.'

LESSONS LEARNT

- It is all very well extolling the benefits that flow from extending negotiations, but, while you are delaying the purchase, think how much fun you are missing by not having the use of the boat. Is that so smart? Life is short. Any week without a boat is a week of life wasted
- One of the big mistakes in life is to negotiate too hard. I must confess I blanch a bit when visiting some third world country and see a comparatively wealthy tourist bartering madly away with a native over the price of some trinket. The rich tourist knows it is half the price it would cost back home, but nevertheless will go back and forth forever quibbling over a few dollars. Must be that beating a poor native down to his last cent is fun. They certainly like to brag about it. These people are the most likely to ironically exclaim in the next breath that the surrounding market area is disgusting. Small wonder. We've banned most blood sports and so we should ban this one as well. So, when negotiating, walk softly, but carry a big tiller.
- If buying the boat privately, check the vessel's ownership and that it is not encumbered in any way.
- To make it a good deal there should be something in it for both parties. This is especially true when buying a boat. By not beating the vendors down to their knees, you can be surprised at all the sudden extras you might win. A well-disposed seller can often find things at home that used to be on the boat that he really has no use for anymore.

- Even more beneficial is the knowledge suddenly and willingly shared. Little secrets like how to get the best out of your new lady, how to handle her, and other little whims and ways.
- To learn your new craft's foibles a friendly word can save you hours of frustration and potentially help avoid considerable expense. For instance, 'Sometimes in shallow water the depth sounder momentarily plays up a bit and gives you extraordinary unlikely depths.' This means, in fact, you're hitting the bottom. Now that can be really useful!
- Take your own photos of the boat to remind you of the real perspective.
- Don't forget the essential importance of a survey. Engines should also be checked over by a qualified mechanic.
- Before the survey, it is best to reach an understanding on the type of issues which may or may not be corrected at the vendor's expense.

TWO

If all this negotiating is not to your liking, then there is another solution: build your own. Let's call this the solution of last resort.

The trouble with most boats built in a backyard, is they look as though they were built in a back yard. However, if you decide you have the skill to beat the odds, go ahead. Firstly however, before you even think of converting that patch of lawn or veggie patch into a shipyard, before you lay even a single plank, or the tiniest first step of keel, think beam. Now go check the width of your driveway and compare that to the planned beam of your new yacht. Simple. Don't snort like that.

But have you remembered to add on the width of the necessary trailer to get it out of there? Forgetting this has seen a few home built boats fail to even sniff the sea. You see them from time to time abandoned in backyards. What a sad sight they make.

One poor fellow got into a right mess. After two years of toiling in his backyard, the boat was finished, paint shining, all antifouled up ready to hit the briny. The big day came and with delivery truck on its way, friends and neighbours crowded around: champagne flowing, little petit fours being nibbled, and stories being exchanged of daring voyages to come.

Excitement mounted as a heavy, flatbed vehicle arrived and, with lots of help and advice from the crowd, managed to squeeze up the drive into the back garden A previously arrived crane successfully loaded the boat onto the truck's flat top. All looked good. But when the truck began to drive out, there came frantic screams to stop.

The boat, beamier than the truck, was sitting at a new height and crashing its topsides into the casement windows of both the owner's house and the ones on the house next door.

While our plucky builder was trying to placate his frantic wife with tales of how the house would look better with a flush window, the next-door neighbour was proving none too cooperative. Poor fellow had to send the truck back empty while he tried to disperse the crowd and calm his hysterical wife. For months he wrestled with solutions: going out through the back was no help and having a crane big enough to lift the boat over his two-storey house required the removal of power and telephone lines and would be more expensive than the boat. Solving the problem was too much for him. In the end, he sold his house …with the boat still in the garden!

Scrounging the Materials

If you're building yourself, it helps if you are a good materials scrounger.

My dad was good at making deals. When he decided to build our first boat it was soon after the World War (No, dear reader, the Second, not the First, and, I'll have you know, I was in short pants.) Shortages and rationing continued in Britain long after the fighting was over and building materials were both hard to come by and, even if you could, they were very expensive. However, thanks to the numerous visits of the Luftwaffe, there was a staggering amount of demolition and rebuilding to be done.

At first bombing was a hit and miss affair. The first bomb casualty in Britain was a rabbit. English music hall veterans

Flanagan and Allen had a huge hit with a derisive song entitled *Run Rabbit Run* in a bid to avoid 'Hitler's little gun.' However, the derision eventually gave way to the true horrors of The Blitz.

While we cannot claim to have been situated at the epicentre of the Battle of Britain, our green and empty fields were amongst the last on the English coast that the German pilots cleared when heading home. In the Third Reich, going back with ordnance still on board was a bit of a bad look. Thus, for honour and glory, it was best no bombs were left.

So, after finishing their raids on London and Southampton and hastening home, they let fly everything left over on the last vestiges of coastal English countryside. Therefore, our hedgerows and fields nightly received a right peppering. Good British hedgehogs suffered horrendously.

Thus, it was not that remarkable that one of these bombs had hit fair and square upon the building next to my dad's office. Fortunately, no one was injured. About three years after the war, a work crew finally turned up to complete the demolition and begin a new structure. Being a friendly, although wily chap, my dad chatted up the foreman and thus scored some of the old timbers. Over a few days he wheeled them home on his bicycle. Although they were charred on the edges and peppered with rusty nails, they were just what dad needed. He pulled out the old nails to melt them down for their metal and then cut and planed the beams to build the framework for a twelve-foot sailing boat.

We also had the good fortune to have a downed Messerschmitt in our back garden. This was not altogether unusual as the Royal Air Force and its Spitfire pilots kindly provided the English countryside with quite a few. Having a downed aeroplane in your backyard was as common as having a couple of garden gnomes.

At the time of the German plane's delivery, we were out. Handy that. Though not for the German pilot. But he had been kind enough not to mess up the cockpit by opting to parachute into a nearby field and hide behind some cows.

While British gunners had begun some great recycling work on the airplane's fuselage while in the air, dad gleefully finished the job by using parts to make a back fence, and here comes the real bonus, metal for making fittings for the new boat.

For a centreboard, he managed to get hold of a steel plate that had been used to construct a strong room in one of the other numerous bombed buildings around our town. But no matter how hard he searched; he could not find enough good planking for anything but the bottom.

In the end, to clad the stringers, dad managed to get hold of some hardboard. Hardboard? This was pre-Masonite, and it was made by hot pressing wastepaper. Basically, it was little more than thickly compressed cardboard. And the trouble with that was when wet it literally disintegrated. All in all, not the ideal material for cladding a boat. However, dad figured that covered with sufficient layers of paint, it should hold together before pulling the boat out at the end of the season for winter. And if it had rotted through, you then just had to slap on some more hardboard.

That brought him to another problem. Again, due to the massive war re-building program, paint was also expensive and hard to get. However, dad lucked onto a builder who was over-stocked with a lurid and bright green paint no one seemed to want. Therefore, he was only too happy to give a couple of cans away in exchange for a pint at the local. The paint was vivid and almost luminescent, and positively called for the boat to be named *Lollipop*.

As I was four and my brother John was eight, dad opted for some very high topsides to stop us from falling overboard. Small she might have been, but out on the water she stood out like the *Queen Mary*.

There was no money or material for sails, but the local Sea Scout troop would sometimes lend us some to use as a standing lug rig. Otherwise, dad would row us around. He taught us all about boating. First, we were only allowed to row with one oar each. Only when we had mastered this, did he allow us to graduate to using two.

Within a few years, we were allowed to take *Lollipop* out on our own. Charging my older brother with my care, dad always severely warned him not to bother coming home without me.

Out on the water, my brother and I were not trusted with the Sea Scouts' sail, so we had to improvise. We used to spend an hour rowing up against the wind and then rig an old curtain to sail downwind. We used one oar to fly the square sail and the other to steer. The journey back only took a few minutes, but we thought it was pure heaven. Then we would laboriously row upwind again to repeat the experience. It was at this tender age that I first learnt to hate going to windward. Life becomes so much better, when cruising through life, if you have a fair wind behind you.

Blowing a Boat Up

Despite the materials used, *Lollipop* lasted for more than twenty years. Of course, building your own boat at home has become much simpler and the choice of materials is now both varied and accessible. We have progressed through marine ply to fibreglass and aluminium. In fact, back in Australia, a friend of mine, who works as an inventor, had a light bulb moment and added a new ingredient: Gelignite.

Don Richardson had worked in the USA's aerospace industry and was across high energy rate forming of metals to impart compound curves into metal sheets. Technical that. Well, it is rocket science. But Don thought that if you could use this technique to economically and repetitively form spaceship parts, why not use it for yacht hulls? Basically, it was the same thing, but on a bigger scale than ever attempted before.

About thirty years ago, Don took the idea and created a breathing steel female mould for a thirty-five feet aluminium hull. The mould was then sunk into a pit in the ground and planar aluminium sheeting welded inside. This rough hull outline was then filled with water. With me so far? Right. The next thing to do was to create a high-energy shock wave that would force the preforming up against the curved mould surface. This technique works because if one hits metal fast enough, it forgets it is metal and forms like a soft plastic.

At this stage Don talked of the highly important act of strategic explosive placement, fuses, and all sorts of other technical stuff. Thank goodness he's not a terrorist. But I like to think of it as simply chucking in some Gelignite and boom: one instantly, perfectly formed hull.

Having worked all this out on paper, Don applied for patents, secured funding and even an Australian Government innovation development grant. Managing to persuade a government to part fund a boat? You can't do better than that! However, the idea had the potential to revolutionise the boat building industry.

For his boat design, he approached the talented Australian yacht designer team of Peter Lowe and Ben Lexcen. Ben was a real character. In his early boat racing days, Ben went by the name of Bob Miller. He then went into the chandlery business with a partner, and as Miller's name was well known in yachting circles, it quickly prospered.

When Bob left the business, his former partner would not relinquish Bob's name from the chandlery store fronts. So, Bob said if he won't change the business name, then I will change mine. He asked a friend who worked at *Reader's Digest* what was the least used name on its list of thousands of subscribers. The answer was Lexcen. Next, he changed his first name to Ben. This was in honour of his dog.

As Ben Lexcen, he went on to build an even bigger name for himself. He was most famous for being the man who designed Australia's successful America Cup Challenger with its secret winged keel. After 132 years of American dominance, Ben played an enormous role in making Australia the first country to ever wrest the Auld Mug from its revered position on a pedestal in the snooty New York Yacht Club. They thought they would never, ever lose it.

When asked what they would put in that hallowed case if the club did lose the cup, the answer was very succinct: the head of the person who lost it.

Coming down to the last and deciding race of the Australian challenge in 1983 was a big moment in the world of yachting. Boatloads of journalists and TV cameras were covering the event for live TV. It was breakfast time in Australia and Australians were stuck by their TV sets holding their breaths. There was no doubt, a lot of people were going to be late for work that day. In the last leg of the race Australia maintained its lead and did win.

The whole country went mad. Next to appear on Australian national television was the Australian socialist Prime Minister, Bob Hawke. Like all good socialists when given the opportunity, he was merrily clasping a brimming glass of champagne in his tipsy hands. Leaning back, he declared, 'Anyone that sacks somebody for not turning up for work today is a bum!' Aussie politicians can be so statesmen like. However, bad as some are, they could still teach a little decorum to Donny Trump.

Ben himself seemed to take the final Aussie winning of the America Cup quite calmly. When asked what he was going to do with the huge ornate silver trophy, he said he would drive over it, flatten it and rename it the Australian Plate. In Australia, that's called being 'dinki-di.'

So, it was no surprise that Ben insisted the new boat being exploded out of its mould for Don should be called *Gelignite*. Come the big day for the forming of the first hull, eager lookers-on joined Don's high-energy rate forming (HERF) engineer, flown in from the United States, multitudinous government officials, health and safety officers, TV crews and other media. They all eagerly assembled around the pit. As the big moment came, everyone cautiously stepped back as special high-speed cameras, running at 6000 frames per second, were set filming to ensure nothing scientific would be missed.

A button was pressed. And boom! Up went an enormous water geyser. After everyone had wiped the water out of their eyes, mopped up their clothing and regained their hearing, they looked down into the ground and there, right in front of them, was a perfectly formed aluminium hull. It took less than a second. This is a true story folks. You can even see it for yourself on You Tube.

The drenched health and safety guys, while awed by the mighty explosion, began to wet their knickers at the idea of all that gelignite floating around the boating industry to mass-produce boats was a step too awful to contemplate. Even before Al Qaeda reared its ugly head, the mere thought had their timbers more than shivered. Sadly, as a consequence, the entire concept was nixed.

However, Don did end up with a beautiful Lexcen designed, lightweight, stiff and sound yacht. Pundits claimed the hull would not last five years, but Don proved them wrong by happily sailing her for the rest of his life.

Unless you have a secret stash of gelignite, this is one building technique we have to say, 'don't try this at home'.

If building your own seems to be too much of a hassle and you can't afford to buy off the peg, the only solution left is to buy lottery tickets. It works for some, but never for me.

Which is a pity as I have always fancied the idea of being a winner and then being interviewed on the tele. I'm fed up with seeing winners saying, 'This won't change my life a bit. I will carry on living in the same house and keep right on working in my job. I might take the weekend off to visit my aunt in Blackpool, but otherwise my life will go on just the same. Nothing will change.' I ask you, what a dreamless lot! Why the bloody hell did they buy a ticket in the first place?

My fantasy of winning is for the satisfaction of fronting the cameras to say, 'This won't change my life a bit. However, I will buy out my workplace and fire all those blighters who gave me a hard time. My present home is very cosy, and we have lived there for twenty years. Thus, I will keep it... for my wife. For myself, I will engage a team of architects to build a brand-new, waterfront, playboy mansion with tennis courts, a golf course and space for my new super yacht at the end of my own jetty. While my mansion is under construction, I will take a luxury world cruise in first class. Other than these minor adjustments, my life will continue just the same.'

Now the chance to do that would be real fun. Wouldn't it?

Quirky Tells a Story

Quirky, our magnificent illustrator for this book, told me this story:

Many years ago, a little girl was sent to stay with her maiden aunt during the school holidays. The aunt lived by the sea but as it rained nonstop, beach activity was out. During a break in the weather, the little girl strolled around the waterfront and found a shed where some men were working on a wooden boat and were about to build another. They offered her a cup of tea. Afterwards, she washed up all their cups and cleaned up the sink area. Then she swept up all the wood shavings and kept the place tidy while the men explained how they were lofting the lines of the mould for the new boat. They explained the building process of building and what they were doing.

The little girl was delighted to help out and made tea and to keep the place neat and tidy as the moulds were marked, cut out and set up while awaiting the planking. At the end of the week, she was given twenty dollars as a gesture for her help.

The aunt was delighted that the child had been so industriously amused and asked what she would do with her wages.

'Start a bank account,' she said.

So off they went to the bank where the aunt introduced her to the bank manager.

'It is very good that you are starting to save so young.'

said the manager. 'How did you earn this?'

'I worked in a boat shed, helping the men who were building a wooden boat. We did all the lofting from a table of offsets, made the moulds, and set up the stations. Now we are ready for lining off.'

'My goodness, you have learned a lot,' exclaimed the manager. 'Will you be boat building next week?'

The little girl, with her newfound wisdom, said: 'I will if we ever get the f******* timber for the planking.'

The Wisdom of Ernie

I try to sneak past Ernie at the yacht club bar. But it is too late, he has seen me sneaking along in my boat work clothes with sandpaper and scraper in hand.

'Ha!' he said, 'Do you know how to make a yacht look younger?'

Warily I shake my head.

'You give her boat-tox.'

I groan, but that only encourages him. He immediately asks me what are the most dangerous vegetables on a boat?

'That's easy,' says I. 'Everyone knows bananas are bad luck'.

'Nope, that's fruit,' he says: 'Leeks'

He calls after my retreating back, 'If your boat is sick, I know a great dock. It's pier-reviewed.'

I hastily shut the door behind me.

LESSONS LEARNT

- Unless you have tons of experience, it is best to have proper plans for your new boat. If you are building a one-off rather than a class boat, get a naval architect to draw up some plans for you. Building a boat in your garage and making it up as you go along results in a boat that looks just like that.
- Choose your building materials carefully. Let's call the most common the five deadly sins. They are:
- Wooden boats have many admirers, particularly in the last century. It is still popular with connoisseurs, chief of whom are Teredo worms. However, if gluing and screwing is your thing, this is a good way to go. Benefits will include developing strong-arm muscles from all the bailing you will have to do for evermore. However, bailing can be minimised with copious layering of epoxy. Thus treated, you know it's going to float. This is a big plus. Boat builders using concrete should take note of this.
- If you fancy yourself as a bit of a welder, then steel is a good option. The big advantage is you can bang into a few rocks or a coral reef with relative impunity. Properly welded, there will be no leaks and to fix up any dents, all you need do is pop below and bash them out with a hammer. Care must be taken with any metal fittings you add to ensure electrolysis doesn't make the whole boat fall apart. While you will have no need to spend a heap of time on your knees with your bum in the air clutching a varnish brush, you are likely to spend similar time in

the same position but with wire brush and rust killer.

- Aluminium is again a material best tackled by somebody handy at welding. However, although steel is more knock resistant, aluminium is around forty percent lighter. While steel is fire resistant, aluminium is not. This little fact should be remembered by those who like to smoke in bed. To save weight, often aluminium decks are added to steel hulls. But the joining of these two metals requires special welding techniques to stop them falling apart. Beware, expert advice needed.

- Fibreglass is sometimes called GRP for Glass Reinforced Plastic, also as Plastic Fantastic and Tupperware. Take your pick, but remember whatever you call it, it is the most popular boat building material today. The basic concept is that you lay against a mould a glass fibre weaved fabric and then saturate it in a liquid such as polyester resin or epoxy. The first hurdle is the mould. Start by building your hull inside out. Great fun. But it will have no other use if you are building a one-off. More wisely, either rent or buy a mould already built. You must also get the chemistry and temperature of your materials exactly right. While you might not get Teredo worms, the finished hull must be one hundred percent watertight. Otherwise, water will seep along all the fibres and cause a condition known as osmosis. If it were your body, you would call it cancer.

- Concrete might seem an unlikely material to float, but it can, sometimes. Relatively simple to use by anyone with a wire fence and a concrete mixer, it has resulted in some of the ugliest boats ever built. Able to be used by anyone with a backyard, that is where you will mostly likely find them. There they sit, propped on beams and in various stages of completion, sometimes forever. Those that finally launch onto the water, still look like a boat built in a backyard. With concrete, it is likely to inflict more damage to a coral reef than itself. However, in case of collision, be sure to carry a bag of ready-mix concrete. Also be prepared to deal with the dreaded concrete cancer. But don't let me put you off. After all, a yacht racing fraternity managed to successfully build a beautiful, race winning, eighteen metre racing yacht out of ferro cement. She was promptly nick-named the *Flying Footpath*.

WHATS IN A NAME
CHOOSING SOMETHING SWEET

THREE

What's in a name? As far as boats are concerned: everything! The first question always asked is what are you going to call her? Once named, the tradition of the sea is the name is entered into the register of that hairy, royal deep god of the sea, King Neptune, or as the Greeks like to call him, Poseidon. Himself, no less.

Now, sailor folk lore has it that His Royal Highness is very particular about his ledger and will abide no trickery or crossings out. He has proclaimed, 'So she is named, so must she stay.' Obviously, a bit of neat freak.

Failure to observe this rule of the deep can lead to the most tragic of consequences with both boat and owner likely to end up in Davy Jones' Locker. However, in spite of all this, I did once rename one of my boats. I had bought a fine yacht, but across her stern was emblazoned the name *Saucy Sally*.

Unfortunately, I had been previously engaged to a saucy girl named Sally. So that name just had to go. Not to have renamed her would have led to a fate far worse than anything Davy Jones could have dished out. However, I did feel that, given the circumstances, Davy would have understood and put in a good word for me.

I settled on the name *Miranda* as this was the name of my first boat. This was presented by my parents as, when I reached eleven, I was the only one in the family without a boat of their own. I'm not quite sure if I chose the name after Shakespeare's character in the Tempest, or if it was after the cute pet monkey featured in Enid Blyton's popular Barney series. I suspect it was for the latter, but all these decades later, what the hell?

For my daring name change, I followed all the guidelines for those foolish enough to attempt this perilous task. Firstly, I removed the offending name from the stern, lifebuoys and any other items, before moving onto ceremoniously burning all clothing, such as hats and t-shirts embroidered with that dreaded name.

Once every trace of the original was obliterated, I moved onto the recommended step of making a sacrifice to the chief god of the seas. I was unable to find any guidance on what would serve as a suitable sacrifice. Google failed me.

First, I thought of tossing a dead fish over the side. On reflection, a mortal choosing to kill off one of the King's own subjects was maybe not the best idea. And, anyway, if His Highness wanted a quick snack, he had plenty of fish to choose from. Just possibly he was sick to death of fish dinners. I mean once a week on Fridays is okay, but breakfast, lunch and dinner, every day of the week! I ask you.

Maybe I should throw in a nice juicy steak? He could then mix it up a bit. If he was so addicted to fish, he could quickly knock up a nice surf and turf for dinner.

Finally, I remembered he liked gold doubloons. After all, he had collected a whole store of them. Sadly, gold doubloons are a bit hard to come by these days, but I did find some look-alikes. They were embossed gold foil wrapped over chocolate. Just the thing. So, in they went. I do hope he has a sweet tooth.

Launching Ceremonies

When I was a lad, a hundred years ago, we christened our boats. Living in the western hemisphere, we christened everything. In fact, the Crusaders had long insisted on it. But in these politically correct days, boat christening ceremonies are a thing of the past. Lest some are offended, we have naming ceremonies instead. And that includes the Royal Navy. They too, no longer christen but 'name' their ships. The odd thing is they still prefix the name with HMS, for Her Majesty's Ship. And whether it's a Him or a Her, they are still the big boss of the Christian Church of England. Go figure.

Another tradition at naming ceremonies is to smash a bottle of champagne against the bow just before she takes to the water. I'm against this. You'll regret it too if your boat is made of fibreglass. It doesn't do a wooden boat much good either. In fact, unless your boat is made of steel, I would forget the whole idea. It's a dreadful waste of champagne. Just anoint the bow with a little trickle and drink the rest yourself.

Under no circumstances should you steal a leaf out of the book of those Grand Prix car racing types who wildly shake big bottles of the genuine French stuff until the cork pops and champagne sprays everywhere. Damned heathens. No wonder they keep crashing. Serves 'em right!

Can you use a male name for your boat? Traditionally, boats and ships are referred to as 'she', but I guess, in these more gender fluid times, it's not a deal breaker. In fact, the US Navy has named many of its destroyers and aircraft carriers after blokes. And who's going to argue with them?

That brings us to celebrities and royalty being picked to be a vessel's god mother. This has in recent years become common practice in the cruise ship industry. I suspect this is not to honour some long-ago forgotten nautical tradition, but more of a PR vehicle to get a few more column inches in the newspapers. And we shouldn't begrudge them a little self-gratification, should we? After all, when home alone, we all do it.

If they are really into Nordic traditions, next they'll be

putting huge, bare-breasted figureheads on the bows of their ships. Now there's a thought. However, it has not escaped my eagle eye, that on sunny days, some in the small boating community are already managing to inveigle a lady crew member to fulfill this role.

The advantage of a live one, unlike a carved wooden figurehead, is that there is no need to slap on another coat of varnish at the start of every season. This is not to suggest there would be any cost savings.

If you are buying a class boat, sometimes, the list of names to choose from is quite difficult. This happens where there is a tradition of using a name that pays homage to the name of its class.

For example, people owning boats in the dinghy racing Finn class, are encouraged to include the name Finn in the name of their boat. Hence boats come up with names such as Dolphin, *FotoFinnish, Finnale, Finnesse, Beefinn, Finnalist, Finnadict, Finnicky, Finnegan's Wake, Financial Disaster* - you get the idea. A few hundred boats or more later, the task gets a tad tedious. I doff my lid to the bloke that came up with the simple name of Huckleberry.

On the marina, there was a boat called Scholarship. When asked what the owner studied, he said nothing; but he had bought the boat by spending his children's university fund.

If you ever need to send out a distress call, the name of your boat is the first thing to come into play. Because of the frequent dubious quality of radio transmissions, boat names should always be chosen with this fact very much in mind.

The Silliest Boat Name

The silliest example I have come across was named *Say That Again*. Imagine the joys of calling a shore station with that name.

Another fellow I know named his boat *Idunno*. He had built her himself and during the months it took, passers-by would keep asking what she was going to be named. His answer was always 'I dun' know' and the name stuck. But it was hell to use on ship-to-shore radio. The shore station would say please repeat your vessel's name. And back would come the answer: *'Idunno'*. This made for very tedious communication.

One more practical fellow called his boat, *Doctor's Orders*. Then if a work call came in, he could always say he was away on doctor's orders! But imagine radioing a marina asking for a pen for the night when your boat is called *After Berth*. Suddenly, the name is not so clever. Equally, it is important to have perfect diction when calling in as *Piece of Ship*.

An example of radio misconception arising out of a naming issue was raised by Philip Delhunty, in *Afloat* magazine. Philip would sometimes loan his Cessna floatplane to the local Volunteer Marine Rescue group. This valiant band of souls operate in much the same way as the Royal National Lifeboat Institution in England and the Auxiliary Coast Guard in the States

While his plane was being flown by a co-pilot friend, Philip received a phone call from the headquarters of Marine Rescue. Being a government organisation, this is naturally located by the government town planners nowhere near the sea. It is located miles away in Canberra, the national home of government and bureaucracy. Many think Canberra was designed by God's own town planner. Who else would create man with a major recreational facility next to a sewage works?

But the Canberra maritime authorities were on top of their game and knew of Philip's services. They called to tell him they had just heard on the distress channel that his plane was making an immediate sea landing.

Later investigation revealed that the pilot was bringing in two passengers wanting to join a large catamaran moored at Sydney's exclusive Palm Beach. The waiting catamaran was called *Catastrophe*. Get it? *Cat-astrophe*. Clever that, isn't it? Maybe not.

Making his final approach, the pilot used channel sixteen

to hail the catamaran to make ready to receive its visitors.

'*Catastrophe, Catastrophe*', he called, 'This is Cessna Float Plane landing at Palm Beach immediately.

Hearing this, the emergency services went into immediate emergency action. Unaware of the frenzy being scrambled, the floatplane pilot off loaded his passengers and flew blissfully away.

In the south of England, I have been told there is a yacht at the Arun Yacht Club called *Passing Wind*. About ten miles to the west is the Looe Passage, around Selsey Bill. The story is that when the boat was sailing through this passage, a crew member was hit by the boom and the skipper called out the coastguard to get the wounded person ashore quickly. Asked for their name and position, back came the answer, 'We are Passing Wind, in the Looe.'

I really don't know whether or not to believe that one, but it does go to show that when naming your boat, you should bear radio work in mind.

Here is a list of names that, all in all, are probably best avoided.

A Wave From It All
Aloan At Last
Aquadesiac
Aquaholic
Aquaphile
Aquatherapy
Bail Me Out
Bankbreaker
Barely A Wake
Beeracuda
Breaking Wind
Buoy Oh Buoy!
Chicken Ship
Cirrhosis Of The River
Clairebouyant
Costalotta
Court A Sea
Courtship
Current Sea
DeckADence
DelaCaSeas
Devocean
Divorce Sail
Docked Wages
Dream 'N Scheme
EggsTaSea
Flotus
For Sail By Owner
Fore Sail
In Decent Seas

What's in a Name: Choosing Something Sweet

In Deep Ship
In2stoxNBlondes
Infatyhomable
Irish Wake
Keel Over
Knot 4 Sail
Knot Paid IV
Knot Sailors
KnotACare
KnotAYacht
KnotToKnow
Laundered Money
Let's Get NaughtyCall
Lottayot
Lunasea
Mayday
MarraTyme
Maid of Plywood
Moby Dept
Moor Often Than Knot
My Lag
Nausi Viii
Nautibuoy
NautiByNature
Nice Aft
Never Again 2
Paid 1V
Para Docks
Passing Wind
Pier Pressure
Unsinkable 2
Reely Nauti
Sail La Vie
Sails Call
Salty Dawg
Scene Ilse

Sea For Two
Sea Sikh
Sea U Late Oar
Sea Ya
Sea-Battical
Seaclusion
Seaduction
Seas The Day
Seas The Moment
Sex Sea
Ship For Brains
Shipface
Sin Or Swim
TaKeelLa
The Codfather
To Sea Or Knot To Sea
Tomato Sloop
Unorthodocks
Vitamin Sea
Wave Me Goodbye
We'll Sea
Weather Oar Knot
What's Up Dock
Whatever Floats Your Boat
Y Knot?

LESSONS LEARNT

- Simple clear names are best for what is often crackly radio communication. This could be very important in an emergency.
- To avoid confusion, go for simple spelling.
- Make sure the boat name you choose is not offensive. Your mates might think it great fun, but boldly emblazing it on your transom, may cause unnecessary offence.
- Equally, a boat name is something that often ends up being embroidered on hats, and jackets, so make sure you choose something that looks good.
- Remember also, your vessel's name will be recorded on your vessel's papers, insurance documents and EPIRBs. If you must change it, not only respect the laws of the deep, but also make sure you update the details everywhere.

ANCHORS AWEIGH

AMUSING THE ONLOOKERS

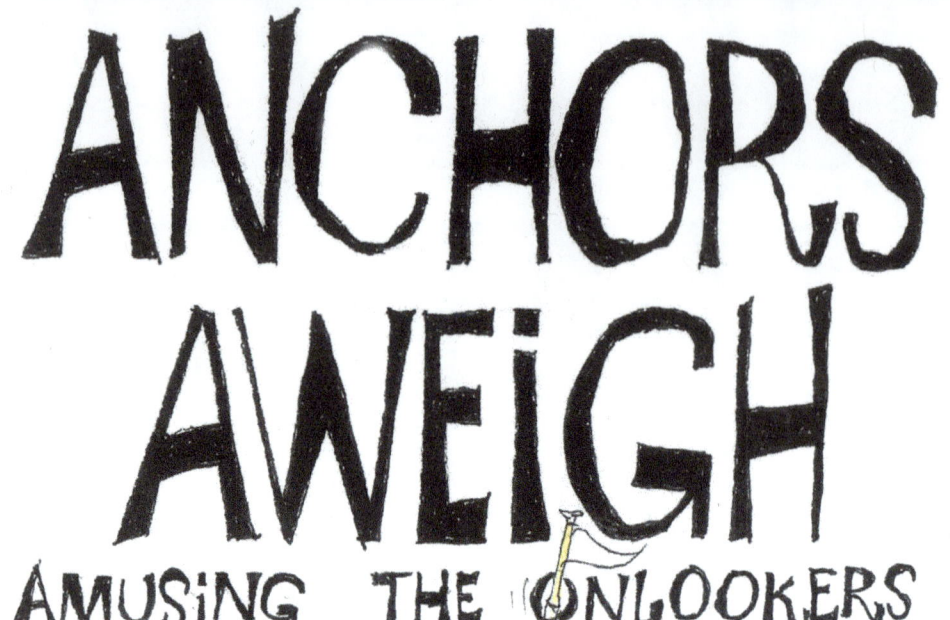

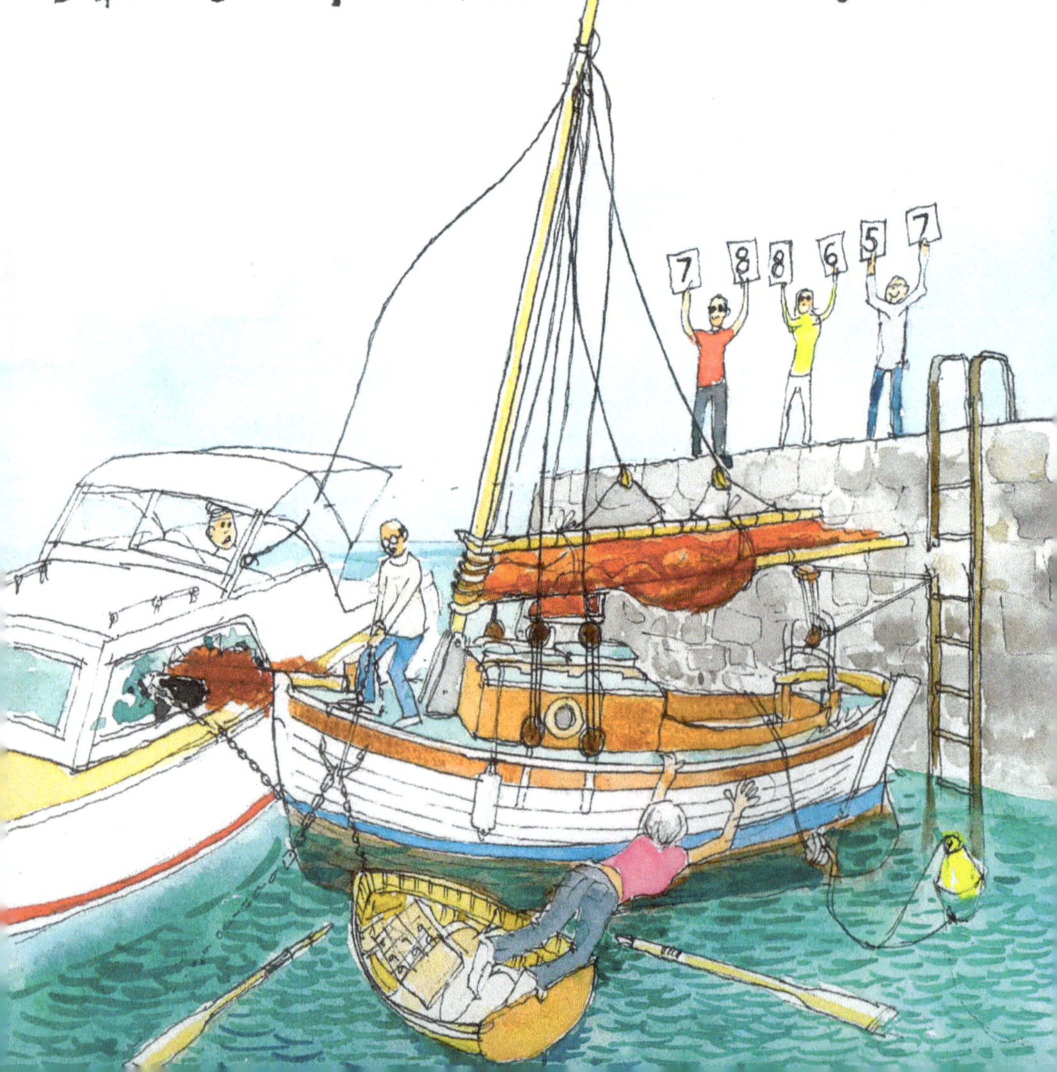

FOUR

Having taken delivery of your splendid vessel, and proudly entered her name in the register of the deep, you're now aboard and in command for the first time. Your mission, should you choose to accept it, is to get underway, hitting as few boats as possible.

Look around. In very close proximity, there are boats everywhere. You are jammed in on all sides. And here's the icing on the cake: people are watching, even betting on your next move. Ghouls. No good waiting. They won't go away. They are always there. Never mind, take a last quick check of your insurance policy and it's time to look lively and make ready to get underway.

On a swing mooring, all the boats normally lie in the same direction, either pointing head to wind, or in the direction of the tide. Or maybe somewhere in between, or maybe, as a bit of a tease, swinging around a bit between the two. As soon as your own mooring buoy is let go, you need to be moving forward smartly to avoid drifting back on the boats behind or to the side. Just make sure your own mooring doesn't get entangled in your propeller. If that happens, your day is over before it has begun.

Sailing off looks very smart and seamanlike but should

only be attempted by those who are very smart and seamanlike. While having to deal with the vagaries of wind and tide, the skipper's view forward is mostly blinded by a ballooning headsail and a flapping main. Keyholes offer better visibility, but franticly yelled steering advice can be heard coming from other boats. They sound dangerously close. Stay cool.

A more challenging departure faces those sardined into the narrow confines of a marina. If you haven't noticed before that marina designers are hell-bent on cramming as many boats into the smallest patch of water possible, you do now. There is less manoeuvring room than in a very tight pair of underpants.

Before casting off, the time has now come to carefully consider the characteristics of the area of the boat hidden beneath the waterline. Maybe, before we finally did the deal with the broker, we should have given this matter more consideration.

When it comes to going astern out of the marina pen, those with a modern light-weight racer/cruiser with deep narrow keel and rudder and prop hanging out, all as free as a nude beach volleyball enthusiast, can zip out with aplomb. However, this hull form is not so much fun in a huge following sea or when entering a foaming, barred river entrance.

Those of us who have gone for the sensible and sturdy full-length keel, protectively housing both propeller and rudder, are going to find things a tad more interesting. Unfortunately, the long keel can require around three boat lengths astern before beginning to gain steerage way. Alas, you would be lucky to find a marina built to allow for that.

At most marinas you will find that just a fraction less than a boat length behind you there is docked a long string of very expensive boats. The more difficult your boat is to steer backwards is in direct proportion to the cost, size, and pure topside gleam of the boats astern. Factor in a lively cross-breeze and you are potentially in for both a spectacular and expensive time. Add into this equation the difficulty of safe manoeuvring is directly multiplied by the number of interested onlookers. But we can't be afraid to leave the marina, can we? So off we go.

Have you ever played pinball and sent a little metal ball bouncing and colliding around banging into colourful illuminated targets? Ping! One thousand dollars, ping: two hundred and fifty dollars. Ping, ping: five hundred dollars…and so on. Well, this is exactly how it can be when backing out of a marina pen. Wind and tide can suddenly make everything go pear-shaped.

With long keeled boats, when breaking inertia for your first thrust astern, it is vital to have the bow at exactly the right angle. For the single hander, this can be quite a challenge. By the time you have released two springs, then ran to the bow lines, then sprinted aft to let go the stern lines and tumble into the cockpit to grasp the helm your boat has already blown into the craft alongside. Ping: Two hundred and fifty dollars! Then the real pinball game begins as you bounce off one boat's side to the stern of another and then rebound onto the boats behind: ping: one hundred dollars; ping: five hundred dollars; and ping: two thousand dollars. Not a good start to your day. There is nothing worse than being totally demoralised before you even start.

I knew one lone sailor who on windy days, just before making a marina departure, would tie-off all his mooring lines with short lengths of wool. Thus, weakly secured at the right angle in his pen, he could calmly go back to the wheel and give a sharp thrust astern. The wool would break; the lines would drop into the water and off he would go. It took him a good fifteen minutes to set up but saved him a fortune in insurance claims.

Returning to the Marina

If you thought leaving the marina seems a bit of a drama, wait till you come back! That lovely 10 knot north easterly wind you had when you left this morning is now a blustery thirty knot south westerly wind. Oh joy. If you have fancy bow and stern thrusters great, but don't expect too much from your stern ones. They never seem powerful enough when a decent breeze gets up. And using the noisy thrusters at all is a sure way to focus everyone's attention in the marina on both you and your anticipated undoing.

On my local marina, a bloke turned up with a brand new shiny Beneteau. Real proud he was. But every time he came back to the marina, he found one of his neighbours had dinged his beautiful new toy. In desperation he went to the marina office and asked for a mooring so he could get away from all the marina madness.

Alas no luck there. He was dinged another few times. Back he went in tears to the marina office seeking some form of salvation. They looked at all their mooring charts. They had just put in new pontoons, rejigged the berths and added extra berths. That gave them an idea.

'We know', they said, 'We will put you next to old Paul. He comes in and out all the time single-handed and has been doing it for thirty years with never a problem.' So, the deal was set.

Just a few days later I was coming in under a stiff breeze and was not yet familiar with the new marina setup. Sizing it up, I got it wrong. The wind blew me down sharply onto the corner of my berth, pivoting my bow round and disastrously pushing through one of his lifelines and slightly bending a stanchion.

Aghast, I went up to the marina office and asked for the contact details of the new boat next to me. Somewhat snootily they said they could not give out any details of fellow berth holders as that information was confidential.

'Okay', I said, 'Could you please ring him and tell him I just hit his boat.'

They blanched and the two of them behind the counter went into a huddle and then left to consult with the marina manager. The upshot of all the urgent whispering was they thought the job of telling the owner of this new catastrophe was best left to me. They quickly wrote down his name and contact details and wished me luck.

I made the call. He was the bigwig managing director of a multinational company. I was having some trouble getting through. His staff were acting all protective and wary. 'What's it about?' they wanted to know. I told them it was about his boat.

With these magic words, they put me straight through. When he answered the phone, I told him how sorry I was and that I would quickly arrange for a new lifeline and of course pay for the work to be done.

In the stunned silence that followed, I anticipated he was gathering himself for a response of utter fury. 'Really,' he said, 'that's amazing. Wonderful.'

'What!' I gasped, 'You don't understand, I hit your boat!'

'Oh yes, I understand, but this is amazing. I've been hit many times. But you're the first bugger to fess up!'

After that, we became good friends and marina neighbours for some years after.

I had another marina upset when I hired a motorboat to take my office out for pre-Christmas drinks one year. I was known for sneering at motorboats, but it seemed the best thing for an office party. So, swallowing my pride, I hired a flybridge cruiser. On returning to the marina, I could see the police, who moored their large seagoing motorboat next to my yacht, together with a few of the other marina wags, all standing on the marina balcony and jeering at the sight of me on the flybridge of a motor cruiser. Cries of 'left hand down a bit' and 'lost your sails' came ringing across the water. For some reason, it was a sight they found uproariously funny.

Unfortunately, in my ignorance, in my final approach I had not properly jigged the twin throttle control down below into dead neutral before I had gone up to the flybridge to get a clearer view for a come alongside. So, when I went to hit reverse for a natty swing into the marina, nothing happened. We just ploughed on. Straight into fifty feet of police boat. They didn't arrest me. They were too busy wetting themselves with laughter. That was the worst punishment of all.

However, they had their revenge. A few weeks later, they crashed into my dinghy hanging on my davits. I don't think they did it deliberately, but I reckoned it was then even-stevens.

Of course, motorboats, especially those with boat and stern thrusters, generally moor stern to. That makes their departure very easy. It's when they return the fun starts.

If you've ever wondered about the many happy crews sitting on their boats in the marina, merrily barbecuing and drinking the day away without ever dropping their lines, after these tales of mishaps, you now know why.

Passing Ernie

I was passing Ernie, our yacht club comedian, who always sits on his stool at the corner of the club bar. Ernie has a fifty-five-foot wooden motor cruiser called *Cash Splash*. Now retired, he goes aboard and potters happily about her without leaving the marina. Lunchtime beckons him to take up his spot at the corner of the bar. Here he stays for the rest of the day.

Members passing from the car park to the marina usually take the short cut of walking through the club. Sitting at his corner, Ernie is a bit of a navigational hazard.

He beckons me over, points out the window at a whole row of boats moored stern to and said I should call the police about them. Puzzled, I stupidly ask why.

'Well,' he said, leaning back and pausing for effect by taking another sip from his schooner, 'They are all being held to transom.'

Dropping the Hook

Once out of the marina we are liberated, free and easy to enjoy all the pleasures of the boating life: tacking and gybing to our heart's content. Eventually, someone will say, why don't we stop for lunch. Well, we managed to deal with the difficulties of getting underway, but now we come to the challenge of stopping. Seeing a good spot, you proudly and nautically proclaim 'We will drop the hook'. Welcome to the joys of anchoring.

The chain and anchor can be dangerous beasts and occasionally you will see someone on the bow holding an anchor and preparing to pitch it out as far as they can with complete disregard for the fact that the anchor line has a few coils around their legs. I've tried shouting warnings, but so intent are they on getting a good throw, they rarely seem to hear. However, I have no trouble hearing their cries as they either disappear overboard with the chain or scream frantically as the chain round their legs bites in to break the fall of the anchor.

I suspect, that in my lifetime of boating, I have managed to make all the anchoring mistakes. Forgivable, maybe, but some of them I have made twice. Whether your boat is small or large, there are, sadly, many different ways to get in trouble when anchoring.

I think back to when I was just a mere lad and out crewing for my brother in our sixteen-foot sailing sharpie. The sun was shining, the breeze kind and gentle and, fancying a swim, we came in under sail to anchor at the beach. The idea was for me to jump in, and make sure we didn't hit the shingle beach too hard before smartly marching up the pebbles to bury the anchor. Simple.

Standing on the bow, with anchor and coiled lengths of chain grasped ready in hand, I looked down into the crystal-clear water. With all that sparkle, the nearby sewerage outflow couldn't have been working that day. When I considered the water to be knee-deep, I jumped.

At that point, my brother said I just simply vanished. It took me a moment to realise where I was: standing on the seabed with two feet of water over my head. Confusing. How come I'm standing under the water? Shouldn't I be spluttering up to the surface. But here I am, perfectly upright, still firmly grasping anchor and chain.

Then came the lightbulb moment. I decided to drop the

chain and anchor. It was the right decision. Bursting rapidly to the surface, I coughed and choked the water out of my lungs. My brother looked down over the side and frowned. 'Best get that anchor,' he said, 'It's no good there.'

We can have so much fun riding securely at anchor while watching other boats attempting to come and do their own anchor manoeuvring. With all the entertainment of boaters making an utter hash of it, you become reluctant to leave and stay all day.

I have one friend who, tinged with a streak of sadistic humour, used his boat to lure unsuspecting yachties onto a sandbank. He had a 45-foot ketch, a beautiful traditional yacht with one unusual design feature. Instead of a long deep keel, she had a centreboard, which just like in sailing dinghies, could be lowered, or raised. This allowed him to anchor his big yacht in water not much more than knee deep.

His weekend mischief was, with his hidden centreboard raised, to anchor close into an attractive beach. There he would bob in happy seclusion. Sooner or later, some stranger would arrive and seeing a big yacht moored in tight to the beach would think, if he can moor there, so can I. The invading boat's forward movement would be suddenly arrested when they hit the unexpected sand bank. My friend would snigger, go below to fetch another beer, and then pop back up again to await his next victim.

The Mediterranean Moor

Let's be perfectly clear here, I am not referring to a member of the Andalusian civilisation but rather the very uncivilised practice of attempting to join a jam-packed, long throng of boats moored stern to a Mediterranean town quay. There's only one way to enjoy this delinquent berthing process: sit at a Greek taverna, attempt to enjoy a glass of ouzo, and watch all the boats coming in and attempting to execute this manoeuvre. Then, finish your drink and head back to your good hotel.

The basic idea of the Mediterranean moor is to festoon your boat with a too sparse collection of vertical hanging fenders on both sides. To me, this is probably a bad start as the fenders could most defensively be deployed by hanging them at a sideways slope and thus quadruple the length of protection. After all, you need as much of this as you can get. The next stage is to turn your stern to the quay, drop your anchor and then hit astern to force the fattest part of your boat between the boats on either side.

This squeezing in process of new boats cheek-by-jowl is akin to a mob of students trying to see how many they can crush into a Toyota Yaris. You then take up residence in the cockpit to enjoy drinks and dinner. A fender width away people in boats either side of you are doing the same. You can enjoy each other's conversations.

Don't worry about this intrusion on your privacy. The worst goldfish bowl experience comes from the hundreds of people walking along the quay to gawk at you.

But it is in the morning the real fun begins. This is when one of the boats decides to leave and discovers their anchor is now trapped in a macrame of other boat anchors. This leads to the unexpected, simultaneous departure of the two boats moored either side. Eventually, the combined weight of the anchors, coupled with gusts of Mistral wind, drags the tangle of three boats into the rest of the line. That's when the yelling starts.

The English favour a different approach to berthing at town quays. They come alongside. Simple. A boat comes in, fenders up and moors alongside the quay. So good, so far. However, the next boat comes in and moors alongside the first. The crews might not know each other, but let's hope they become friends. Then the third boat arrives and so on until you have a line of boats that just about cross the harbour completely.

A sleepless night follows. In the wee small hours, various sailors return from the pub and other revelries to swing across the lifelines and thump across all the decks to reach their own boat.

An early start is guaranteed as after a sleepless night, the second boat in the line seeks to extract itself from the raft up to leave the rest of the line floating loose around the harbour. That's when the yelling starts.

In Norway, the fjords can be so deep that you would need to carry ten tons of chain just to reach bottom. Being a stoic lot, they take to hammering steel rings into the cliff face and tie their boats to those. But with freezing wind and on a bobbing boat, hammering can be a bit of a hit and miss affair and in the process many a Norwegian has suffered a crushed hand. That's when the yelling starts.

In the Caribbean, crime, theft, robbery and drug runners are becoming a major concern. It's wise to pick your areas carefully. At anchor, and even in some marinas, it is advisable to leave a bright light shining in the cockpit and be sure to lock the cockpit door when going to sleep for the night. Sadly, there are now bays where it is not safe to be the only boat in for the night. That's when the yelling starts.

Gun Play

It's important to choose the right place to drop the pick. There is an art to it. However, it seems many weekend boaters have skipped that chapter in the seamanship manual. The results can be both amusing and worrisome.

One beautiful summer's weekend I was peacefully anchored in the lee of a peninsula headland. With this narrow headland there is an ocean beach on one side and a beautiful peaceful beach on the lee side. It's a small but popular anchorage with boaters.

On this particular day, it was blustery and approximately thirty boats were already jam-packed into this tight area. It was shallow water over a thickly weeded bottom. Just paying out a ton of road was not much help: you had to make sure your anchor was deeply dug through the layers of seaweed.

We had all succeeded in doing this. The wind was bulleting down the hill in thirty knot gusts, but the sun was shining, the sky was clear and every one of us was securely settled. Wine was flowing and prawns being eaten.

Suddenly, squeezing into our midst came a large motor cruiser, noisily snorting and veering into the wind gusts. There was much shouting over loud music between the skipper on the bridge and a gaggle of bikinis and budgies on the foredeck. It was quite an entrance. We all looked on more in wonder than in lust. But look, he's preparing to drop anchor in the middle of us all. Where on earth was he going to find swinging room?

Apparently, it was about one boat length directly upwind of me. I heard the chain begin rattling through their hawser. Obviously, he was going to drift right back on top of me. In a flash, I was out of the cockpit and dancing on the foredeck, wildly pointing my arms in any direction that was nowhere near me.

The skipper, resting enormous folds of his bare belly on his steering wheel, hastily decided he didn't want to be close to such a frenetic lunatic. He did some more wind veers and blew sideways out of the anchorage. We all breathed a sigh of relief and returned to our peaceful contemplations.

But next minute, he was back again, weaving through the surrounding boats and attempting to repeat the same procedure in front of another yacht. The skipper, clearly from the same tribe as me, perfectly replicated my dancing and shouting routine. Again, the huge stink boat veered off.

Then, in another five minutes, low and behold, he is back, readying to pitch his pick in front of yet another boat. By now we are all standing fearfully on our foredecks with boathooks and fenders at the ready. Within seconds there was a chorus of shouts, a sickening thud, a clash of topsides and more shouting and heaving as the crew of both boats scrambled to fend off. After a bit of wrestling to free from each other, he motored off again. That, we thought, was the end of that.

Unbelievably, a few minutes later he was back, unchastened, a demonical glint in his eye and a face set grim with determination. He was hell-bent on dropping anchor somewhere. His guests seemed unfazed, ostentatiously sipping champagne and passing around trays of nibbles and canapés. But a heavy cloud of impending doom was descending on the rest of us.

Spying an old weather-beaten sloop, with an equally old weather-beaten, bearded guy barely visible over his coaming, he sized it up, and again we heard the anchor chain start to rattle through the hawser. He probably thought somebody like him would be less pernickety about who was anchoring next to him. Wrong.

We more seasoned folk could see that this was a very experienced sailor who had crossed vast oceans. A slight clue to this was the long line of jerrycans lashed along the rail, baggy wrinkles all the way up the shrouds, an Australia courtesy flag streaming from the starboard crosstree and a German ensign fluttering from the stern.

Like a jack-in-the-box, a huge, bearded skipper unravelled himself from his slumped position in his cockpit, ducked below and, in an instant, magically popped up on his foredeck, legs braced wide and pointing a huge shotgun straight at the intruder.

That brought an instant result. In a flurry, the motorboat jammed its throttles wide open, with anchor still swinging against the bow, it roared out of the anchorage, leaving us all wildly rocking in a huge wake. This created an emergency for me: I had to quickly dive to save my wine.

Peace and lunch resumed. But fifteen minutes later, a police boat appeared and began to gently nose through our little moored flotilla. Spotting my boat and knowing me from sharing the same marina, they came alongside for a chat. Basically, they wanted to know which boat had the shotgun. In an attempt to signal my fellow boaties, with much theatrical shrugging of the shoulders and shaking of the head, I played dumb. To me, this comes quite easily.

Giving me an intense stare, the police moved over to the

next boat and were obviously asking the same questions. They gave an encore of my performance. Slowly the police motored from boat to boat, asking the same question. Apparently, no one saw anything. At around the tenth boat, some rotter squealed, and an accusative arm went up pointing to the German boat. The police then moved directly alongside, disappeared below to reappear with the shotgun and put it into the police boat. A moment later, they remerged with the owner and put him into the police boat as well. They then motored off.

When I returned my boat to the marina and I was coming up the ramp to the car park, I saw the sergeant leaning over the balcony and slowly wagging a knowing and reproving finger side-to-side at me. 'Oh,' I say, looking all innocent, 'I saw you taking him away. Was it to give him a medal?'

Picking Up a Buoy

Another endless source of entertainment for those already moored, is watching another boat coming in to pick up a buoy. As a rule of thumb, it seems the more people helping on the foredeck, the more disastrous the result will be. There is much pointing and yelling and eventually the mooring slides under the boat to wrap itself a few times around the prop. Now they are more anchored than moored.

When it comes to just a husband-and-wife team onboard, this splitting of assignments makes no sense at all. It's blowing twenty knots and here they come on their twenty-ton motor cruiser. They are still at some considerable distance, but you know they are looking to pick up a mooring as there is the lady of the house already up on the foredeck, determinedly poised with a boat hook.

The wife waves the boat hook in the general direction of a buoy and if she is very lucky, the big muscly husband at the wheel turns the boat to approach from an upwind or up-tide direction. When they approach with the wind broadside on, we know we're in for a real show.

Once the mooring is neared, there then follows a period of mad yelling of instructions between foredeck and flybridge. The voice of the wife becomes more strangled and fainter as she leans further and further over the rail to try and hook the buoy.

She's got it! But now here comes a gust of wind veering the bow off and leaving her stretching and pulling on the rope to try and drop it over a cleat. She has obviously been missing her muscleman training sessions as she is now at the stage where she cannot unhook the buoy and has to decide between releasing her grip on the boathook or being pulled with it over the side of the boat.

Meanwhile, whilst this epic struggle of strength is going on, the big strong man tiddling with the controls, is wildly yelling to hurry-up.

This misallocation of roles, based on some strange idea of gender, is totally beyond me. A woman is perfectly capable of driving a boat and surely it should be the man that is sent to the foredeck to do the heavy lifting.

If the woman is the stronger of the two, all well and good, but in any event the pair should practise hand-signal recognition between them. Failing that, if they both have mobile phones and earbuds, they could communicate with each other that way. Just please stop all that shouting. Let those of us moored nearby have our afternoon naps in peace.

Ernie Again

I tell this story to Ernie, the comedian in the yacht club bar: 'Reminds me,' he says, 'of the skipper who was hunting around a crowded anchorage, searching for a place to drop the hook before dark. There was no room anywhere and there was nowhere else to bed down for miles. Looked like he was in for a long night at sea.

'Looking up to heaven he prays, "Oh dear Father, my lord, take pity on me, your humble servant. Find me a good spot and I will give up the demon drink, pay my taxes and never again yell at my crew."

Miraculously, the boat with the best spot in the bay starts pulling up anchor to leave. The skipper look up again and says, 'Never mind, I found one myself.'

The Need to be Close

Sometimes, no matter how much room there is, a boat comes along and anchors directly on top of you. What's with these lemmings? I'll tell you a story.

Making passage alone, after a family holiday amongst the islands of the Great Barrier Reef, I anchored for the night in a very lonely spot behind a big island which opens up from protected waters to the South Pacific.

Between the two is a long and sometimes dangerous bar. Planning to cross on the next day's dawn tide, I set to, stowing all the loose things I had left lying around in our three months inside the calm waters of the reef. After I secured everything below, I turned my attention to my dinghy which swung low in its davits. I lifted off the outboard and fuel tank, and just to be sure, removed the dinghy from the davits, hoisted it up onto the foredeck and lashed it securely into place.

Finally, with everything ship-shape for the more boisterous seas ahead, I settled self-satisfied into the cockpit with gin and tonic in hand to watch the sun go down. It was an ideal time to contemplate such weighty matters as how deep would the ocean be if sponges didn't grow in it? Or why it is that when transporting something by lorry it's called shipment, but when transporting something by ship, it's called cargo?

Thus, mindfully engaged, I idly watched as another sailing boat hove into view, working her way along the long and empty stretches of the lee island shore. Looked like she was cruising along looking for a good anchoring spot. Eventually she found one: just a few feet in front of me.

Why? I mentally shrugged my shoulders and watched a

lone sailor pottering around his foredeck. He had been towing an old aluminium dinghy behind, but now he pulled it alongside his neglected topsides and was fiddling with long lengths of line and electrical cord. He popped out of sight for a moment and then reappeared lugging a portable petrol generator. He started it and dropped it still running into his dinghy. The noise and fumes shattered the peace and freshness of the evening air.

My mouth gaped open as he proceeded to pay out the dinghy's long painter and electrical cord until it came to end of its tether. It was now over my anchor. The dinghy, with its roaring and smoking generator, was less than a boat length in front of me. He tied it off and promptly disappeared below. Incredible.

I sat stunned. No way could I tolerate that noise and smell all night. Spurred into action. I did my foredeck dancing and yelling routine until my feet were raw and my voice was hoarse. There was no movement from the other boat. In desperation, I reluctantly unlashed my tender, connected it to the halyard and lowered it back over the side. I then unstowed the oars.

Fifteen minutes later I had undone all my bar crossing preparations and as I rowed over to his boat, I was not happy. I hammered on his topsides until my hands were raw. Eventually his face popped out of his cabin. He cupped his hands to his ears as virtually speechless I wildly pointed to his dinghy with generator roaring away like a Boeing 747 on take-off. "Sorry,' he said, 'But I can't stand the noise of that generator.'

Fortunately, I was not armed.

Chucking Anchors Overboard

I met one family with a boat that had no anchor at all. They were a family of five, a husband-and-wife couple and three children ranging from four to ten years old, and living on a boat, moored opposite us on a marina.

The boat had to be seen to be believed. She was looking

very backyard built, with something like a milking shed serving as a coach house. She was very beamy and around forty-six feet long. The construction must have required a whole fleet of concrete mixer trucks. The sweep of the deck looked like an off-ramp on the Pacific Highway.

Below, there were no cabins. It was just an enormous empty void, pierced through the middle with a mast like a telegraph pole going right through to the keel. A dozen or so pipe berths lined the sides and along the sole were littered an assortment of various sized open suitcases, serving as drawers for the family of five. They were full to overflowing and spewing their contents higgledy-piggledy onto the floor. A few plastic chairs were scattered about along with a trestle table supporting a primus stove. At this stage she had three anchors.

The family had been living in the West Australia city of Perth. One day the husband, tiring of his job as a plumber, decided to take a break for a few years and try out this boating game. Although he had never gone sailing, he had heard much about it and thought it came highly recommended.

The family agreed it all sounded rather fun, so with each family member carrying two suitcases, they took the six-hour flight to Queensland's Gold Coast. Straight off the plane, the family took their suitcases and scattering of shoulder bags into a broker's office and asked to see some boats. The broker, very much doubting a potential sale, showed them three boats suitable for a family of this size. The last one they liked and the man of the house, opened one of the suitcases and counted out the full price in cash into the astonished broker's hands. Explained the wife, 'We had to have somewhere to sleep that night.'

Two days later, they set off for their first-ever sail. Having got out of the marina and out to sea, they were none too sure of the process for getting back. So, they decided to get on with their trip and headed north.

They sailed through the night, but their forward progress was cut short when they clipped a reef. They dropped the anchor, got on the radio, and called the rescue service for a tow. The rescue boat arrived and duly hitched them up. When they came to pull up the anchor, they found it was caught on the reef, so they let the lot go, chain, rope and anchor. No, they hadn't thought of buoying it first.

After another night in port, they pressed on. When the time came to anchor, they dropped the one lashed to the second bow roller. When it came to go, the wife merely cast off the chain and, being untied, it fell straight to the bottom. She thought that was what one did.

During the day, they progressed up the coast, but come nightfall, the weather turned a bit rough, so they called up a local rescue boat for another tow in. After a couple more days in port, they determined to continue their voyage. At the end of the day, they pulled out the last spare anchor and chain and dropped it over the side. The chain slithered through the anchor rollers, but before it could be made fast, the bare end quickly disappeared into the sea. Still, no one had thought to check the anchor was tied to the boat. With no anchors left, they got on the radio and again called out the local rescue boat.

Chatting to me on the marina, the husband said how great he thought the marine rescue service was. 'All you have to do is call them up on the radio. They come very promptly. It's just like the national automobile association.'

No, I didn't know it was like that.

He also told me he was not buying any more anchors. 'With the chain and all, it's too expensive. From now on, we are just going to use marinas.'

Over the next couple of days, we noticed the boat coming to and from the mainland to the island marina. They always seemed to have lots of visitors aboard. It turned out that to make a little extra cash, they had put up a homemade poster on a local backpackers' noticeboard boldly advertising two-day trips to the island for half the normal charter price. To my horror, they seemed to be doing a roaring trade. All very illegal and with no insurance.

The wife learnt from someone that I was making my living as a journalist. She came across one day to tell me that she had just taken up writing and was recording their journey for an article she hoped to sell to a yachting magazine.

'Would you mind,' she asked, 'casting an eye over the manuscript for me.'

I very reluctantly agreed. Lured over for evening drinks, the wife retrieved a sheaf of closely typed pages. As I read of all their adventures as complete novices, my jaw dropped open wider and wider in amazement at the sheer audacity of what they had been doing and wondering how on earth they had survived.

Tentatively, she asked, 'Do you think a yachting magazine would publish it?'

'I don't know,' I said, 'But they ought to!'

Plumbing the Depths

British architect Roger Pinckney was a well-known boating figure and the owner of a beautiful yacht named Dyarchy, which he kept moored at the mouth of the Solent's Lymington River. She was based on the classic British Pilot Cutter and off the drawing board of famous yacht designer Laurent Giles. She had flush decks and very little headroom. Roger's philosophy was that if you wanted to stand at full stretch, you should go up on deck.

Dyarchy was very seaworthy, forty-six feet long, and weighed in at 24 tons: not the easiest thing to manoeuvre in a congested and narrow river.

One day, during his tenure as Vice Commodore of the Royal Lymington Yacht Club, he rounded up under full sail in front of the clubhouse to come alongside the club jetty, But due to the narrowness of the river, instead of coming alongside, he ended up at right-angles to the club building, hard on the mud and with the bowsprit hanging over the club's sea wall.

Roger was not going to admit anything had gone wrong.

With great aplomb, he calmly stepped off the bowsprit, dropped down and took the six steps to enter the club's committee meeting room.

Local legend has it that thereafter Roger got carried away with this idea and used to repeat the manoeuvre with great success when visiting a pub on the nearby Hamble River. This had a suitable mud bank directly in front of the pub to arrest *Dyarchy's* forward momentum. But one time, Roger forgot it was high water springs.

When *Dyarchy* rounded up her bow, she went over the mudbank and hit the sea wall. The bowsprit, higher than the wall, went straight through the pub's window and knocked a pint of beer out of a startled drinker's hands. A local wag leaned out of the window and shouted at Roger, 'If you're coming in any further old chap, we're going to have to move some of the furniture.'

Here Come the Jet Skis

Having mastered anchoring, it must be said there is absolutely nothing finer than gracefully executing this manoeuvre off a secluded and small, sheltered sandy beach. Again, cruising the Barrier Reef islands, we came across just such a bay.

Dropping the pick a couple of cricket pitches from the shore, we sat in the cockpit and admired a thatched beach bar. It was catering to a dozen comatose drinkers blissfully and sleepily lying in hammocks strung between the palm trees. Paradise.

Into this peaceful scene drove an enterprising young man in a pick-up truck with a trailer carrying two jet skis. He set up a folding chair and a sign advertising them for hire. Soon the peace was shattered with the sound of roaring engines as they mindlessly circled the small bay and sent their wake slapping against our hull.

The only difference between a jet ski and a vacuum sweeper is the location of the dirt bag. And the difference between a jet skier and a big bucket of poo is just the bucket. They are not branded Sea Doos for nothing.

You can see, I'm no fan of jet skis. But back on the beach, a line was forming to take their turn. I got into my dinghy and rowed across to chat to the operator.

'How much,' I politely queried, 'do you hope to profit from this day's activity.'

He thought for a bit and came up with a figure. We then deducted the cost of fuel and wear and tear on his equipment. This brought the answer down to fifty dollars.

I opened my wallet, pulled out a fifty and told him to take his bloody noisy contraptions and piss-off. And looking very happy, he did.

This was a couple of decades ago. Now the jet ski operator has a fleet of forty jet skis continually running around the whole island. These days, I couldn't even think of buying him off! But I wish I could.

Jet skis and screaming children remain my bête noir. I don't mind jet skis at all when they are used to go from point A to point B, but all this endless going around in noisy, wave making circles and endless donuts drives me mad.

When I started working on ocean passenger liners, I liked the rumble and hull shaking roar of the huge anchors being let go. How the whole ship would shudder as the huge chains ripped through the hawser. Sometimes, I imagined jet skiers and spoilt children going down with it. Many of the children I encountered could be noisier, more objectionable and spoilt than any I had encountered ashore. I used to take perverse inner delight muttering to pesky brat passenger to 'go play with the anchor'. Out of parental earshot of course.

Children can be forgiven, but jet skiers? They remain the reason why, when cruising, I think it best for me not to carry a gun.

LESSONS LEARNT

- Always ensure the end of your anchor line is properly secured to your boat.
- Rather than using a shackle, it is best to tie the end with a couple of rounds of strong cord. Then, in an emergency, with a jammed anchor that won't come up, you can quickly cut your tackle free with a sharp knife. No, not that: the anchor tackle I mean.
- If you have snared your anchor, don't just let the anchor go without first tying the end of the chain or rope to a marker buoy for later retrieval.
- In rocky places where it is easy for the anchor to get trapped, it's a good trick to tie a buoyed line directly over the top of your anchor. That way you can easily give a jammed anchor a reverse pull. But keep an eye on it in case some clown comes along and tries to moor up to it. Painting a warning on the buoy is a good idea.
- Remember, when anchoring over coral, it can quickly chafe through anchor rope, so it is best to use all chain.
- Don't forget to let out plenty of anchor line. A good rule of thumb is to let out seven times the depth plus the height of your freeboard.
- Read up on the different types of anchors, rodes lengths and snubbers. There's lots to learn. It's best to do it!
- If you're picking up a mooring in windy conditions and you're shorthanded, it is a good idea to first run a line with a clip on it back to your steering position, outside

of all rigging etcetera. Then you near the mooring from your steering position, hook it up, clip on, then go forward to pull the line in. No screaming necessary.

NAVIGATION AND PILOTAGE

FIVE

Now we come to the mysterious art of navigation. He was by no means the first, but nevertheless, Captain Cook was a bit of a trend setter in this department. He had a couple of compasses offering different opinions and was geared up to measure latitude and longitude. But a vital part of his navigational arsenal was a sharp watch and an acute ear. Near land, all ears were peeled back for the nightmarish sound of breaking surf on rocks. Bit like my mum. She used her ear for reverse parking in shopping centres. If her ear failed her, she would fall back on her sharp eye to see the car behind slowly rising on her bumper.

Nor was Cook immune from using this technique. On several occasions he plotted submerged reefs with this very method. Wisely, Captain Cook sailed sturdy ships with particular attention paid to the strength of the bits under the water line. And to his credit, much of the charts in use today owe much to his diligent plotting.

There are many clues to position fixing. A mad keen racing mate of mine was on a long race and looking to pick up a fast-moving current in their direction of travel.

Finding the current causes a notable increase in sea temperature, so the navigator kept popping up from his navigation table to drop a thermometer down a cockpit drain hole. One of the lads, it was lads of course, thought it was great fun to pee down the drain hole and then rouse the navigator. Up came the navigator, dropped down his thermometer and excitedly proclaimed they had found the current. He couldn't understand why the rest of the crew were collapsing with laughter.

Pre GPS

Over the years I have looked forward to attaining the distinction of being called an 'old salt'. After all, compared with some of the other things I'm called, this indeed would be an honour. And by way of qualification, I proudly point out that Captain Cook and my humble self both began our cruising lives before the miracle of the Global Positioning System.

Admittedly, I had the advantage of charts, and had no need to make my own. With charts I can plan my cruises with none of the edgy feelings Magellan had when he set out to check if the world was indeed round.

But there was still plenty of room for navigational error as GPS was yet to be invented. When it was first released on the consumer market, as a positioning system, it was incredibly accurate. But in the early days of GPS, the US Government deliberately dithered its signals for fear of a terrorist using it to drop a missile down a White House chimney. That meant to us amateur sailors out on the seas, sometimes we were not quite sure which side of the odd reef to pass.

But now, without the dithering, GPS is so reliable, I can't help feeling it has taken some of the fun and excitement out of cruising. Not only do we know exactly where we are, but even worse, the exact time of arrival at our destination. How boring is that? You might as well be on a bus. Gone is the excitement of making your first landfall to the accompaniment of an unexpected grating noise under the keel.

Being unable to know to the nearest prick of the dividers your exact location, brings a little frisson of excitement, even a sense of achievement. With GPS, it is all so predictable. Yawn.

When making its debut, GPS created much excitement. It was all very wonderful and important: it even made the TV news. In fact, the best TV laugh I ever had was when watching a large trawler demonstrating its precision on a television show. The captain blacked out his wheelhouse windows and then successfully navigated with pinpoint accuracy around four markers set in the bay. As viewers, we sat agog watching the final return alongside a formidable stone quay. Executing a flourishing broadside thrust, the vessel hit the quayside, beam-on. There was a sickening crash. The TV camera jumped a bit, as did the captain. Busted ribs for both boat and crew. He had forgotten his GPS, rather than being located on the port side gunnel, was in fact 10 feet away amidships of his beamy vessel. What a catastrophe. Hilarious that.

Mind you, I once did something equally dumb. My son and I were sailing the Great Barrier Reef and tired, late at night, we decided to anchor up behind an island and get some rest. As most of the islands have a swell curving around the lee side, I tried to pick a spot with the least amount of roll. This was in the early days of GPS which only gave you your lat and long. You then had to transfer it to a paper chart and mark your position with a pencil.

With my son on the foredeck peering through the darkness, we edged up ever so carefully behind a reef which would protect us from the swell. Struggling to stay awake, I kept carefully transferring our positions to the chart until we were just a smidge behind the reef. We dropped anchor and retired for the night. Now the tide in these parts can rise and fall by about ten metres. In the morning, we were shocked to see a boat length ahead, the reef towering above us. I had been so carried away with the new technology that I had forgotten that even the width of my chart pencil was more than two boats lengths!

Shooting the Sun

Proper paper charts mostly seem to end up as soggy, tablecloth-sized sheets of paper covered in compass pin pricks and half-erased pencil lines. Today, many boaters have never even seen a chart printed on anything but a tea-towel. But, before flashing digital readouts and glowing monitors, we were totally reliant on paper charts.

By night we attempted to point sextants at impossible to identify stars. Easy enough at celestial navigation school, but it is slightly more challenging on a bouncing vessel heaving through the waves and spewing buckets of water down your neck.

These stars might or might not appear from time to time above the waves or from behind a dark cloud. We would then try to guess which star or planet was which. There's quite a few of them up there. In the city, you don't see much, but when you get to sea, there are thousands of the blighters.

We tried to work out which was which with the aid of a round printed sky chart. On your heaving boat, you were meant to hold it above your head and read it in the dark. This is not an easy thing to do when sails, mast and waves are gyrating everywhere. This is especially true when it's gone midnight, you are feeling seasick and as mentally acute as a soggy lettuce.

Having made your best guess at what you were trying to identify, you next had to consult the small print of your nautical almanac. Bit of applied trigonometry and you're home and hosed. Hope you were better at school than I was.

With all sums sorted the time has come to transfer your position to the chart. Struggling to stay standing, you run your rule along the latitude, bisect it with the longitude and try to jab your pencil as your boat momentarily pauses at the top of a wave. Voila! That is where you are. Or maybe think you are. This circle of confusion is the point on which all other life-preserving decisions will be made. Let's hope it's right.

Some of us found the whole celestial navigation lark a bit hard. But, what the hell, we went cruising anyway.

Keeping to the Left

Navigating the great coastal seas of Australia, the basic idea was if you wanted to go north, you kept Australia on the left. And, of course, vice versa if you wanted to go south. And you prayed a lot. This simple system had the double benefits of knowing that at some time, if you could see the Sydney Harbour Bridge and you kept going, eventually, you would see it again.

Of course, in the daytime, additional positional information becomes available. But have you ever noticed that when viewed from the sea, one set of hills looks very much like another? To help you with this, charts include sectional views of the coast printed sideways along their narrow border. But who amongst your crew could hold up a flapping chart and successfully identify one headland from another?

One might put you twenty nautical miles north. The other might opine it to be twenty miles south. And if you decide to split the difference, there is a reef slap bang in the middle.

Truth is, successfully identifying your position from the landmarks printed on the edge of a chart compares with the chance of finding a vacant mooring in the Medina during Cowes Week.

Nevertheless, firm opinions are formed and thus we come to the first law of visual navigation. With visual positioning, the number of differing opinions is in direct proportion to the inverse square ratio of the number of crew carried on the vessel.

In these dark pre-GPS days, when we were mere blissful novices at long distance coastal cruising, we welcomed aboard our thirty-four-foot sloop a crew of highly seasoned yachties. These were experienced souls who knew every rock and wave on the Australian coast. Or so we thought.

We set off from Sydney aiming for the Great Barrier Reef. We knew we couldn't miss it: it is two thousand miles long. Indeed, Captain Cook hit upon it a couple of times. However, while he carried his own band of repair shipwrights, we did not.

On the second day out from Sydney, with night falling, we encountered a surprise storm front. Don't you love those? The barometer lost its libido, falling as fast as the light. As the waves reached up to towering tongue-shaped, black, omniscient masses, we hastily reefed. The waves built. And built. The deepest dark of night grew darker. The seas pitched steeper, and the wind blew harder. We were near a lee shore. We were confident it was still called New South Wales. It was only our second day out and that coast is more than a thousand miles long. Seeking the safety of plenty of sea room, we drove eastwards away from the rocky coast.

Soon there was not even the flicker of a lighthouse. In fact, we could see nothing at all: not even a horizon line between sea and sky. We were just pitching and tossing around in a world of blackness.

We never did find out how hard the wind blew that night. At fifty-seven knots the wind instruments blew off the top of the mast. But the seas were massive.

It was on this night that I first looked for god. Any god. I tried them all. But she must have been busy elsewhere. Maybe a famine in Africa, a flood in Viagra or whatever it's called, or maybe at a Republican Convention in Alabama? Anyway, we were damned sure she had deserted us as we headed out into mountainous seas away from the hazards of the coast.

As is so often proved, our worthy little boat survived the night better than her crew. In fact, dawn came gracefully, mocking us with her serenity. Seas and wind slipped away softly whispering sorry as they went. They had just been in a bad mood last night. But as the sun came up over the horizon, peeping hesitating through the clouds and showing little enthusiasm for a new day, it cruelly revealed the look of sheer horror still etched on our faces. Sitting stunned in the cockpit, we decided to start the motor and motor-sail back towards land.

Fire!

Immediately, from down below, came wisps of smoke and a smell of burning rubber. We hastily switched off the motor, cautiously cracked the engine hatch open half an inch and took a quick peep. All the pounding we had taken had sheared the fridge compressor off the side of the engine and it had fallen through its own wiring and started a small fire of the rubber insulating the wires. Fortunately, we had a good handyman on board who called for a wire coat hanger, which he used to strap the compressor clear of the engine and tidy up the remains of its wiring.

We got underway again, and two went down below to prepare breakfast. A few minutes later and smoke and the smell of burning comes billowing out of the cabin. Fire at sea twice in the same day? Surely this was the voyage of the damned.

I sprang into full safety mode and moved to cut off all air supply to the fire below. Slamming shut the cockpit hatch behind me, I pushed the breakfast cooks out of the way to reach over and close all the ports and the overhead hatch. Rushing up to the bow, I closed more ports, sprung up through the hatch above and grabbed the cockpit fire extinguisher. Returning to open again the main hatch of the cabin, I found the two cooks still below and not being familiar with the boat, quivering at the fear of having been shut in. They had bad names for me. They rushed out the hatch and left me to deal with the fire. Casting about, I found the source: some bread had dropped to the bottom of the toaster and set itself alight.

After we finally settled down, we were still so far offshore, there was no sign of the coast. So, we turned the wheel fifteen degrees to close it. By noon, there was still no hint of land, so we put our left hand down a bit for another fifteen degrees. Another hour, and still no sight of the coast. We added another ten degrees of left hand down a bit. Ah yes, we were a nautical lot. After another hour of looking at an empty horizon, we decided to hell with it and sailed due west, straight to where the coast had to be.

With sunset and night looming, we were relieved to see at last rolling hills and sweeping cliffs breaking the horizon. Out came the charts, held on their side by the experts who were comparing the sketches on the edges to the vista before them. There was disagreement. A long discussion ensued. My heart sank when I noticed they had not one, but three different charts out! One reckoned we were off Port Stephens, another reckoned we were off Crowdy Head, the other was convinced we were off Port Macquarie – all about thirty miles apart.

By now the glassy calm was shining in the setting sun as we glided along at a stately five knots. Two miles off the coast, a small aluminium dinghy bobbed contentedly. Lines were hanging over the sides and two fishermen were sitting with their eskies, sucking on their gold, glinting beer cans, marked clearly with XXXX. (That's how we Australians spell beer). The sun was sinking fast and all hope of getting an accurate position fix was going with it. Swallowing our pride, we brought our vessel within hailing range.

Adopting a firm nautical stance on the foredeck, I cupped hands to mouth and hailed, 'Ahoy there! Wheere arre wee?'

Having seen our direct approach from over the horizon, both fishermen jumped to their feet, perilously rocking their dinghy. Excitedly they pointed to the hills behind them. 'Oorstralia….. Oorstarlia, mate…. Bloody Oorstarlia!'

Oh dear! They had obviously mistaken our appearance from over the horizon for the arrival of an around the world yacht! How were we to explain that we had not yet come a couple of hundred miles and just wanted the name of the nearest town?

A brief muttered consultation between our crew took place. We made our decision. We gave a brief and nonchalant salute of our hands. 'Merci' we called, 'Merci beaucoup'.

And on we sailed, still clueless as to where we were, but making sure to keep 'Oorstralia' firmly on the left.

Ernie Has a Story

You do not need to go long distance cruising to get into navigational difficulties. Ernie, the comedian in the yacht club bar, has his own story:

A novice yachtsman was going for his first day sail on the Solent: the popular sailing strip of water between the South of England and the Isle of Wight.

He had promised his wife he would be home at teatime, but when it came time to head back, he looked at the low-lying shore, and could not make out the mouth of his river. He sailed close to another yacht, and hailed saying, 'I promised my wife I would be home on time but I'm afraid I don't know where I am. Can you help me?'

The other skipper replied, 'Sure, you are at fifty degrees and forty-five minutes north and one degrees and twenty-four minutes west, in eight meters of water.'

'You must be a Tory,' exlaimed the novice.

'Yes, I am,' said the other sailor. 'How did you guess?'

'Well, while everything you've told me may be technically correct, it was not responsive to the intent of my question and no help to me with my need to get back home. I am still lost. Frankly, you've been no help at all and now I'm going to be late.'

The other sailor sniffed. 'You must be a labour voter.'

'I am and proud of it,' replied the novice, 'but how did you know that?'

Came the reply, 'You don't know where you are or how to get where you want to go. You made a promise that you have no idea of how to keep and you expect me to solve your problem. The fact is you were lost and in danger of being late getting home before we met, but now, somehow, it's my fault.'

LESSONS LEARNT

- GPS is a wonderful aid, but even if only coastal cruising, it is not to be totally relied upon. A power outage on your boat will render it useless. And as surprising as it may sound, technology sometimes fails us. For this reason, it is important to learn the rudiments of position fixing. A hand bearing compass, pencil, ruler and a pair of dividers are a very small investment.

- To estimate the speed of your boat, at the bow, drop over any piece of biodegradable material that will float and time the seconds it takes to reach the end of the transom. Knowing the length of your boat and that one knot equals around one hundred feet a minute, you can calculate your boat speed. The formula is: (L x 60) (T x 100) = V, where L is length in feet, T is time in seconds and V is speed in knots. Simple, isn't it?

- Always make sure you have a proper navigational chart for the area you are cruising. If you travel the same routes regularly, it is a good idea to overlay the chart with a heavy sheet of Perspex so you can mark your position on the Perspex with a chinagraph pencil. Your markings are easily wiped off and the chart always remains pristine clean.

- Even when your GPS is working perfectly, transfer your position to the chart every hour. Then if it does suddenly go down, you will have a good idea of your position.

- If you're going great distances, it's a good idea to buy a battery-powered, handheld GPS unit as a back-up. Crossing oceans, take two!

- Remember, knowing your depth can also help you find your right position on the chart.
- Never come ashore after a bit of a fright at sea proclaiming you are never going out again. Your friends will laugh when they see you returning a week later.

SIX

Once you have succeeded in discovering your position, transfer it to your chart with a decisive stab of the dividers. I notice some tend to close their eyes while making little circular movements in the general area before making that fatal stab.

It is now routine practice to report that position with confidence to a land-based coastguard radio monitoring station. That way, regardless of any wishes relatives and coastguard may be secretly harbouring, they know you have not yet sunk.

However, since Titanic issued the distress call that brought the mighty but little Carpathia dashing through the icefields to rescue survivors of the disaster, the humble but invaluable marine radio has earned its place on any boat. But operating ship-to-shore radio brings a whole new world of potential embarrassment.

Radio work should not be a problem for me. In the 1960s, I was the cabin class entertainments officer aboard what used to be the biggest ship in the world, the *RMS Queen Mary*. Aboard the *Mary*, it was my nightly duty to call bingo, give passenger talks on such things as the number of knives, forks and spoons we carried and host the evening's cabaret show. Oh, you are wondering? Well, it was 3,400 knives, 11,000 forks and 22,500 spoons. Six thousand of the latter were of the highly pinchable teaspoon variety. Fascinating, isn't it?

The rich and famous of the day were not above bumming a free ride by doing their party piece to pay their passage. Hence, I got to compère and introduce some famous show business names of the day.

I had both a black and a white dinner jacket. And I wasn't even a waiter. You can see I was quite suave. I was a professional at the microphone game. It was the nightly tool of my trade. And, as my local paper reported, I had called bingo for Richard Burton, Elizabeth Taylor and Billy Graham, all sitting huddled together at the same table. With microphone in hand, I even dared ask Billy Graham if he was there to marry them…. again! Nothing shy about me. Even after I gave up the ship entertainment game, my work still meant I was no stranger to the microphone as I was quite comfortable doing regular radio and TV interviews.

However, show me a microphone attached to either the boat's VHF or HF radio and the worst attack of stage fright renders me the complete gibbering idiot. Just clicking on the push-to-talk button has my knees knocking like castanets and a voice quavering and creaking like an old wooden mast.

I might only be talking one-on-one, but I know all my fellow yachties are listening in to see if I follow the strict, correct maritime radio procedure and wondering what sort of problem I have that needs a radio call. That's not good for my confidence.

The high frequency band radio is my worst nightmare. That signal skips and bounces to seafarers around the world. Nonchalantly tossing off phrases such as 'Catch up on the HF mate, maybe we can raft up along the way,' may sound all very well in the warmth and security of the yacht club bar. But when at sea, gripping for dear life to a spray drenched cockpit coaming and wind whistling in your ears, you are apt to find things not quite so easy. When the radio is emitting more crackle and pop than a bowl of Rice Krispies, deciphering what is said becomes something of a guessing game.

When I am transmitting, I am imagining everyone within a two thousand nautical mile radius is hearing the transmission with perfect clarity and snorting to their shipboard mates. 'It's that twerp again. What's he doing out there? Can't he see there's a storm front coming?' Or, if in port and trying to get my aerial to compete with several hundred nearby aluminium masts, I imagine I hear, 'Not moving on today? It's only thirty-five knots, what a wimp! And listen to that crackle: he doesn't even know how to tune a radio.'

So, when making my annual two-thousand-mile trek along the coast, my twice-daily H.F. position reports to the Australian Penta Comstat monitoring base were made with great trepidation.

To transmit, I carefully make my preparations. First check no members of the crew are holding the backstay antenna rigging. It's such a pain turning back to recover the burnt-out crisp of a crewman. Then I power up the batteries by running the engine in neutral, anxiously tune and retune the HF radio, knowing all the time I'm sending a screeching sound through every radio in the vicinity. Checking the time, I anxiously await the deep and sonorous tones of Penta Comstat's Derek as he prepares to track his list of yachts meandering around the Barrier Reef and South Pacific. Derek has done this job for years. It's a labour of love. It's not that he's bored. It's just that his natural voice is so laden with gloom you immediately felt the end of the world is at hand.

While some sea radio forecasters can paralyse you with the overly excited mention of a twenty-knot breeze, Derek's very dry and matter of fact. To me his tone would say, 'If you have any boating capability at all, you needn't worry about the cyclonic winds heading in your direction. They will only reach seventy-five knots; the seas will be below seven meters and will ease over the next fortnight'.

Even if his forecast is for light winds and calm seas, somehow, I couldn't help feeling that we were about to be sunk without trace.

Derek alternated with his wife Janine, so you got one in the morning and the other in the evening. Janine had a completely different voice. It was gentle, warm and sympathetic. She was always bright and merry, no matter what. Her tone was, 'Oh, thirty-five knots on the nose again? Well, it's sure to ease off soon.' Her voice had a 'let's- have-fun-but-don't-spill-the-gin' quality.

Calling in Your Position

I'll never forget one very embarrassing day. I am anxiously awaiting my turn to give my daily position report on the early morning sked. It's all done in alphabetical boat name order. I am listening intently through all the interference for my boat name. We went through *Anouk,* whistle pop, then *Beachcomber,* whistle, crackle, pop, through to *Lively Lady,* crackle, crackle, and at last, yes, '*Moiranda*", crackle, crackle, crackle, whistle, whistle pop, pop. *Moiranda?*' That must be us, mustn't it?

I quickly grasp the microphone, even remembering to press the talk button, 'This is *Miranda,*' trying to sound super confident. Steading myself as we lurch down an extra steep wave, I say 'We have twenty-eight knot winds on the nose, nor-by-nor east. (Actually, it's gusting nearer thirty-five, but I do think it's so much more professional to be understated. Don't you?) 'Good visibility (but for the constant spray in my face) and a low swell.' (Here, I pause a moment to vomit over the side…not mal-de-mer…more stage fright.)

I continue, '*Miranda* is currently positioned two nautical miles south-east of Cockermouth Island. Over.'

'Say again,' came the dry voice of Derek.

'We are two nautical miles south-east of Cockermouth Island'.

'Please repeat your position, you are two nautical miles south-east of where?'

'Cockermouth, repeat Cockermouth. Over.'

'Please say again'.

Even through the static, I can discern Derek's voice becoming extra stern. Dreadful realisation dawns. He thinks I am saying what! Am I breaching radio etiquette and a hundred other rules with some form of frivolous obscenity? This transmission is definitely heading in the wrong direction.

My stomach sinks to my sea boots: 'C.O.C.K E.R.M.O.U.T.H.'

Silence! But for whistle, crack pop. Foolishly, I blunder on: 'That's,' I stammer, 'Charlie, October, Charlie, Kilo, Echo, Romeo, Mike, October, Uniform, Tango, Hotel: COCKERMOUTH.' (See, I had been to radio school.)

Derek's voice comes humourless, filled with ominous disapproval. 'I've never heard of that one,' he mutters in a very dubious tone, 'I will have to check the chart for that.'

We then knew, if he couldn't find it, he would never call us again. If you are doubting this story, take a look at a chart of the southern end of the Whitsunday Islands. See? There it is, plain as a gouge in your topsides.

Later that day, in a gently dying breeze, with the setting sun sparking ruby red rays across a sapphire sea, we made peaceful anchorage behind Balls Head. Settling down with our pre-dinner gin and tonics and admiring the view, we decided, given everything, it was probably best not to radio in our position from here.

The Good Old Days of HF

Knowing your exact location is important and it should be transferred to a chart as soon as possible. Once, making a long passage through narrow channels in a protected waterway, I spied a good overnight anchorage behind a small island. It was the worst night of my life. Boeing sized mosquitoes stormed my smoke coil deterrents, determined to strip me to a skeleton before daybreak. It was a night of pure bug-splatting agony.

The next morning, bitten and sore, I pulled out the chart to put in my exact position to ensure I would never anchor here again. But somebody had already been here before me. The little anchorage already had a name, and it was already clearly printed on the chart: 'Mosquito Point.'

Getting back to position reporting, it is not always the boat's transmissions that can be unprofessional. I well remember the night when a government shore station operator was, shall we say, a little the worse for a different kind of weather.

He came late on HF to give the evening weather report. Night had fallen and we were being tossed around in a rising sea. As we anxiously strained our ears to hear his transmission, we realised his speech was slurred and it was obvious he was heavily under the influence. His transmission went something like this.

'Good evening boating suckers. If you've not had the sense to be in port, I guess you all want the weather report. I've got it here somewhere.'

There was then a long period of noisy static and occasional muttering. 'Ah yes, here it is. It was issued somewhere around 1630 hours, or was that yesterday?' Another long pause. 'Oh dearie, dearie me. I'm bloody glad to be nice and snug ashore tonight.' Then came the sound of a bottle clinking on glass and a vigorous slurping sound.

'This is not good fellows; you are in for a rough one.... terrible. No, no, no. You don't want to be at sea tonight. Another long pause filled with static. 'Winds will be from the north at forty-five knots…and rising….no that's the sea….no…. it's both wind and sea. If I were you, I would take shelter fast. If it was me, I would get a shore job. Oh, I'm there already, ha-ha... good luck fellows!'

And there we were, hanging on in wildly pitching seas and straining to hear every syllable in total bemusement. He did answer a few calls from some fishing boats that obviously knew him well. He enjoyed himself by commenting sarcastically and making puns on the name of every boat that called him.

One last word on radio work. A popular nautical yarn,

told to me by Ernie in the yacht club bar, claims to be based on a true incident. It is not. The story has been told for a couple of decades and originally concerned semaphore light signalling. These days it is claimed to be a transcript of a radio conversation. It is still rubbish. But never mind, as every reporter knows, never let the facts get in the way of a good story. Here we go:

The commander of a US navy fleet of warships steaming in battle formation was concerned to see a bright light looming directly ahead. Picking up his radio he ordered the light to divert course twenty degrees north to avoid collision

Back came the answer, 'Negative. Recommend you divert your course twenty degrees south to avoid collision. Over'

Annoyed the commander radioed back. 'I am the admiral of a United States warship. I say again, divert your course. Over'

In came the answer. 'I say again, you will have to divert your course. Over.'

Now incensed, the admiral drew himself up to his full height and bellowed into his radio microphone, 'This is the *USS Gerald R. Ford* and we are the largest ship in the US Navy. We are accompanied by three destroyers, three cruisers and a line of support ships. I demand that you change your course twenty degrees to the north, or countermeasures will be undertaken to ensure the safety of this flotilla.'

Back came the answer: 'You make your own decision. This is the Nantucket Lighthouse.'

LESSONS LEARNED

- I see little need for an HF radio these days. Although some ships might still have them, no one is listening. A sat phone might be a good investment.
- It is important to have a secure way of communicating your position at sea so that family and friends can be assured that you are safe. There are many coastal VHF stations that serve this purpose
- If, when going to sea and you have signed into a VHF station, in the event of an emergency they will already have all your particulars. This could save your life.
- Do not rely on mobile phones to make emergency contact. A flat battery or a black spot could leave you very vulnerable. A VHF radio is a must have for anyone boating offshore.
- Electronic Positioning Indicating Radio Beacons, which do just that and are known as EPIRBS for short, are an essential item for any boat going offshore. Their continuously transmitted SOS message is readily picked up by any type of nearby aircraft, and unless they are flying over an inland rubbish tip where some people foolishly discard their old ones, they will call in your distress signal for you.
- Another recently new addition to radio reporting is AIS. This stands for Automatic Identification System and basically it reports the names of other vessels in your area, their distance, which direction they are travelling and

how fast they are going, along with some other information about the vessel. This is very useful, as with AIS, you will know who hit you.

- Learn the phonetic alphabet, it is not Delta, India, Foxtrot, Foxtrot, India, Charlie, Uniform, Lima, Tango.
- As a reminder, the NATO Phonetic Alphabet is Alpha, Bravo, Charlie, Delta, Echo, Foxtrot, Golf, Hotel, India, Juliet, Kilo, Lima, Mike, November, Oscar, Papa, Quebec, Romeo, Sierra, Tango, Uniform, Victor, Whiskey, X-ray, Yankee, Zulu.
- Numbers are read off as English digits, but the pronunciations of three, four, five, nine and thousand are modified to be: TREE, FOW-er, FIFE, NIN-er and TOU-SAND.

LIVING ABOARD
WHILE SAVING RELATIONSHIPS

Apart from that I rather enjoy cooking with a primus...

SEVEN

Travels with a Cat

It seems all very nice to take the family pussy along when cruising up the coast, but it's not just a question of putting on some kitty litter and rationing up some cat food. They don't just spend their days curled up purring in the cockpit. Oh no. Cats have their own agenda.

Our first mistake was naming our family moggie 'Gybo,' We thought it a nice nautical name that might put some extra swing in his tail for his favourite pastime of marching a marina, imperiously inspecting the other boats.

However, when we had to get him back and call out 'Gybo', you could see all the nearby sailing types quickly ducking their heads and then looking around with a perplexed air.

After I had my ketch completely resprayed and given a facelift even Joan Collins would envy, we set off on a coastal cruise. When we pulled into a marina for a couple of nights, our sparkling topsides blinding passers-by, many stopped to admire and compliment us on our boat's perfection.

The next morning, sitting in the cockpit, I was surprised to see small crowds forming at the bows to admire our boat.

Even women and children were pointing, cooing and sighing aloud before walking on. Boy did I feel proud. But many of the children were laughing and giggling, which seemed a bit odd. I went forward to investigate.

Gybo was lying in the scuppers, poking his paws and head through the hawser, putting on a real show for every passer-by. They weren't admiring my lovely boat at all. It was just the blasted cat!

Truth is, Gybo was not much of a sailor. On nice days at sea, he would disappear completely. A quick search of the boat would have us checking our wake to see he hadn't fallen overboard. However, he would always eventually turn up: tucked away in a furled-up sail, hiding under our bedclothes, or curled up under the dinghy.

If the weather got rough, he would go down into the saloon, spread his legs wide and with head down make horrendous, dry retching sounds. He was never actually sick, but the sight and sound of him could set everyone else off.

At night he could be a real nuisance. We had to keep hatches and doors Gybo-proofed. He was always finding ways to crawl into your bed and stretch out across your neck and shoulders. A real pest. And a real whore. He would sleep with anyone.

One hot summer's night, after returning from a late dinner ashore, we tip-toed back along a very quiet marina and onto our boat. We were all quickly asleep. A somnambulistic trance enveloped the marina. Halyards abandoned their ceaseless rattling to hang still and silent. No water slapped the hulls; hatches gaped open in an attempt to gulp some night air. Utter, sublime peace reigned.

A couple of hours after midnight, the night was shattered by the horrific screams of a woman in a boat berthed nearby. Somebody was being murdered. Springing out of bed I could see the whole marina was lighting up. Groups of people rushed towards a big motor launch: the source of the continued wailing and sobbing. As I approached, I heard a woman cry out in relief, 'Oh, it's a cat! Oh my god, it's a cat!'

Oh indeed. I crept quietly back to my cockpit and laid low. From there, I could clearly hear the full story. The woman, fast asleep under an open hatch, in the middle of the night felt a big ball of fur land on her and stretch itself across her neck. Jerking from deep slumber, in the blackness she didn't know if it was animal or human. Whatever it was, she thought her days were at an end. Oh dear, Oh dear.

I saw Gybo slinking towards our boat and preparing to jump aboard. Not wanting ownership, I waived him off, hissing quietly and urgently, 'Go away! Go Away!'

Marina Revenge

When sailing a long coastline, providing the cruising kitty can cover it, an occasional stopover in a marina is a great convenience. Necessary revictualing is easier when you don't have to lug heaps of groceries in and out of a dinghy, plus you can top up fuel and freshwater tanks and enjoy a night on the town. The best advantage of all, if you don't like your neighbours, you can move.

When you have a mass of boats moored in the confines of a marina, most of us respect our neighbours, converse in low voices, and make as little fuss and noise as possible. However, there are some exceptions. Regrettably, most of these come not from visiting boats, but regulars keeping their boat there all the time and only turning up when they can muster enough friends and family to form a noisy party. To use marinas as party central is all okay within reason, but there are limits.

Late one hot night, a gang of drunkenly merry people arrived to party in the cockpit of a boat just inches away from mine. They were chattering and laughing noisily long past midnight. They had to shout at each other to make themselves heard over the music blasting from their cockpit music system. By two AM, they were still in full swing, and my fuse of patience was being lit. It's a long fuse, and it burns slow. But it is definitely there. When I arose from my sleepless bed at four

AM, it was still dark, but at last it was perfectly silent, save for the gnashing of my teeth.

Normal early morning departure routine is a very considerate affair. I creep around the boat undoing all my lines and only when there is a single line holding me to the marina, will I start the engine, release the line and back out quietly. I take pride in the fact that no one will note my passing.

This morning was going to be different. My heart was filled with vengeance. I was going to strike like Thor. The first thing I did was start my engine and give it a few noisy revs to make sure everything was sweet. Not quite as satisfying as a Harley, but it did a fair job in a marina. I then switched on my spreader flood lights effectively turning night into day for the boat next door. To prolong the vengeance, I made a cuppa and sipped it meditatively over a slice of toast. In due time, I dropped like an elephant onto the marina, and with a merry whistle, leisurely began to untie my lines.

I was now ready to leave, but there had still been no movement from the boat next to me. So disappointing. They were trying to tough it out. There was no way I was going to let them get away with that.

I wrap smartly on their topsides. Still no movement. Determined, I beat my fists hard on the hull. Success! A light flickers on. One more thump and a rag mop of hair emerges, followed by a very hung-over face with blinking bleary eyes.

'I'm off now,' I call loudly and cheerfully. 'Just wanted to say goodbye. Catch up with you next time.'

Satisfyingly, I heard a mumbled goodbye in return. So off I went, with diabolical grin and evilly chuckling to myself.

The lesson here is don't mess with old sailors.

Sex and the Sailor

While the whole family might be up for weekends pottering around the local bays, not all family members might be so enthusiastic about heading off on a passage of a few days and nights in the open sea. I am not saying this separates the boys from the men, or even the boys from the gals, or any of that nonsense. It's just different. The bay travellers may be just fun-loving sensible folk, whereas the ocean goers might be looking for a foolhardy mission to jazz up their boring lives.

I venture to tread warily now upon the divisive topic of whether or not it is the fairer sex who prefer the bays to the ocean or vice versa. However, even though women are generally conceded to be more sensible than their menfolk, such a wide sweeping assumption about women and ocean sailing would be foolhardy indeed.

To prove my point, we need look no further than Kay Cottee, Jessica Watson, Naomi James, Clare Francis and Jeanne Socrates. All ocean goers of great repute. And Jeanne did her circumnavigation at the age of seventy-seven.

Happy is the relationship when both partners like ocean going. Finding such like-minded souls is not easy. But we know they are out there. They write books about it.

A young mate of mine, preparing his boat for a cruise up the coast and then off across the Pacific, was bragging about how he had found the perfect gal. She was coming from interstate, and he was going to teach her how to sail. She eventually arrived and after a few familiarisation trips around the bays, off they went on their big adventure.

A few weeks later, I set off on my own trip up the coast and eventually caught up with their boat. I lowered my dinghy to row over for a social visit. To my surprise there was only the girl on the boat. Apparently, there had been a bit of a fright at sea and the guy had decided he didn't want to go on. But the girl wanted to keep going. She bought the boat from him, kicked him off and continued the voyage alone.

I also met a married girl who had set off with her husband and was learning to sail. Apparently, they had an almighty row in a port and while he was off doing some shopping, she up anchored and sailed off without him. From my conversation, I learned he was now two hundred miles back and she had no intention of returning to look for him.

How Not to Save a Marriage

On my local marina, I made friends with a bloke in the berth next door who was fitting out his thirty-six-foot sloop ready for a long stint of coastal cruising. It was his first boat, but he was an excellent craftsman and worked away all hours of the day and night aiming for the perfect fit-out.

Over a beer one night he told me he was fixing up his boat as his marriage was in trouble. His wife had not sailed before. However, he was convinced that once they started off, with their three young children aboard, the sailing life would have everything coming up roses.

He was planning his trip with great enthusiasm. He told me he would set off at eight o'clock at night, put the kids to bed and they would arrive at their first port as day was breaking.

'What a magical moment that will be!' he enthused. 'Beaches and golden sands, for the kids; sunset cocktails for my wife and me. Doesn't that sound wonderful?'

Wonderful? I was still pondering his setting off at night with his novice wife and children when his own previous sailing experience was a couple of trips out on a friend's boat. Gently, I tried to point out that the sea could be quite rough around the port entrance, and it might be a good idea to first start off pottering around the local bays as a shake down experience for the family.

But he would have none of it. 'My marriage needs this,' he insisted. 'I have to save my marriage. All will be safe. I have done a coastal navigation course.'

My gentle attempt at caution was waived off. So, with the work completed they set sail one night, right on schedule. The first night at sea they had a terrifying experience. With wind and waves kicked up against the current, it was so black they couldn't tell the line between sea and sky.

They were back four days later. By the end of the week, divorce proceedings had begun.

Done Racing

My sailing club had a very active group of young members and both girls and boys joined to get to meet each other and, of course, many romantic attachments resulted. It must have been the sea air.

At this time, before I went to sea on cruise ships, I worked as a press and general photographer and would photograph occasional weekend weddings. Thus, it was that when a young couple of dinghy racers in my local sailing club decided to get hitched, I was invited to take the wedding photographs.

It was quite an honour as this particular couple were the toast of the club. Initially, the husband-to-be had been a successful Finn sailor, but when he began courting, he gave up the single-handed life and bought a racing dinghy for two. His girl entered the spirit of competitive sailing with gusto. They would be out in all weathers, buckets of cold water flying into their faces with the plucky lady drenched and freezing. She was a champion, sitting out and leaning over the side as far as possible, with hands red-raw from clinging onto jib sheets. They were a great team and cleaned up every race.

Come the big day of the wedding, the whole club turned up. As the photographer, it was my job at the end of the ceremony to pose the couple outside the church door. While the rest of the congregation were coming out a side door, I would then set about arranging the long trail of the bridal gown. This put me in a position to hear the first words a couple speak in their newly married state. I heard some very interesting first words, but this one took the cake.

As I fiddled and fussed with her gown, the bride held up her finger, examined the wedding ring and then turned to her new husband and said, 'By the way, that's the last time I go out in that bloody boat of yours.'

And it was.

Passing Ernie, our comedian in the yacht club bar, he calls out to me, 'Hey you used to work on cruise ships, didn't you?'

'Uh-huh.'

'So, you would know what you call a thousand politicians on a sinking cruise ship?'

'No Ernie, I don't know what you would call a thousand politicians on a sinking cruise ship.'

'It's what you call a good start.'

'Goodnight Ernie.'

Going Bananas

Sailors' superstitions are legendary. We have already dealt with the name changing issue, but there are many others. The most common is fear of having bananas on board. This is not attributable to a comedic prat fall sending a crewman flying overboard. The fact is that in the 1700s, at the height of the banana trade between Spain and the Caribbean, many vessels carrying a cargo of banana disappeared at sea.

There are a couple of reasons for this. Firstly, as bananas go off quickly, the boats used to pile on all sails and go like the clappers. This brought increased risks, but there was no money in delivering a load of rotten bananas.

The second reason is the heat in the banana storage holds could cause this cargo to emit dangerous fumes. If the fumes didn't get a crewman, they could be bitten by a deadly spider hiding in the bananas. So, there you are: bananas were decidedly bad luck.

Whereas today it is considered good luck to attract a woman aboard, in yesteryears it was considered bad luck. This was because a woman distracted men from their duties and had the crew competing for her favours. This led to knife fights and sailors falling, or even being thrown, overboard.

Funny enough, sailor superstition had it that naked women on board were entirely welcome. And men could all say amen to that. But the real reason was that it was thought naked women 'calmed the sea'. Only sailors would try and get away with that one. But I doubt it calmed the men.

Perhaps it was for this reason, possibly due to a lack

of sufficient obliging ladies, to calm the seas, sailors took to perching a bare breasted, carved wooden figure head on the prow of their boats.

Today, many of the companies advertising boats seek to continue the practice with ads showing half-naked ladies perched on the foredeck. I suspect this is less to calm the seas, but more to excite the market.

Whistle While You Work

Whistling was also thought to be very bad luck. Not because it was insulting to the ladies, but because it was believed to excite the god of wind. Aiolos, was a Greek god, and while there is no shortage of them, it is a good idea to treat them all with respect. As a consequence, sailors came up with the expression, 'Whistling up a storm.' And we don't want that. Do we?

Another cause of angst among the crew was the sight of a shark following the ship. I have no argument with that one. One slip over the side and you're shark meat. Dolphins, on the other hand, are considered good luck. Presumably because they won't eat you.

Sailors also don't like to set sail on Thursdays or Fridays, possibly because they like to get in a long weekend. The first Monday in April, the day Cain slew Abel, and the second Monday in August, the day Sodom and Gomorrah were destroyed, are also bad luck. Presumably, for the latter, it was an act of unity.

Sailors really believe the best day to set sail is a Sunday. And I wonder if that is because not only do they get to cut church, but also earn penalty rates.

Another superstition meant cutting one's hair, nail trimming, and beard shaving must be avoided at all costs. I like this one. At sea, I have adopted it as well.

If you had ginger hair, then you were bad luck. No reason given, except that picking on people because of the colour of their hair, can turn out to be very bad luck indeed. Red hair was also thought to signal a hot temper. Please, I am only reporting this, I am not endorsing it. But we must know our history. So sue me.

Thanks to poet Coleridge, we all know about the danger of killing an albatross. It's deemed good luck to see a seabird as they are meant to carry the souls of dead sailors. Why that should be good luck is not for us to understand but kill one at your peril.

By now you will be thinking there is not much you can do to avoid bringing bad luck to your seafaring, yet there is more. Using words such as drowned, goodbye and good luck, plus anything to do with land, such as pigs, foxes, cats and rabbits will get ole' Neptune all riled up. Even passing the salt is a no-no.

The approved way to say goodbye to a sailor is to say, 'May you have fair winds and following seas.' And don't we all wish for that one.

One superstition that certainly did me no good, was the habit of putting coins under a mast for good luck. On my Hong Kong built ketch, both main and mizzen wooden masts went rotten at the base as the coins effectively blocked the drainage holes in the mast step. By no means could the cost of replacing two wooden masts with two aluminium ones, be considered good luck.

Shocking Cruising

When my children were very young, I took my family for a long cruise up a river in my twenty-five-foot sailing boat. There was beautiful countryside on either side and no sudden strong winds or waves to contend with. To anchor up for the night, all we did was pull alongside the riverbank. Apart from mud banks, there were no hazards at all. There were bridges and overhead power lines, but I had carefully checked and found we had a good two meters of clearance above the mast for all. What could go wrong?

My young daughter and I had risen early to get underway on the tide. It was another of the week's very hot days and the banks were alive with the sound of crickets and colourful birds: all singing their little hearts out.

We came upon some large yellow signs warning us there were low-lying overhead power lines ahead. The notice also said that if touched with a mast, they carried enough voltage to hurl you into the next century. The lines sagged in the middle and as an extra precaution I held the riverbank very close to clear the power lines at their highest point.

As we neared to go under, my little daughter looked up and said, 'Daddy! Those lines are going to hit the mast.'

I explained in a calm, matter-of-fact voice it was an optical illusion due to our angle of view. I went on to tell her how in 1963, when the Verrazano Narrows bridge was being constructed over the entrance to New York harbour, due to this same angle of view phenomenon, passengers on the Queen Mary used to scream as we passed under. I was the nonchalant, knowledgeable dad. Real cool.

As I was talking, I looked up at my directional windvane on the top of my aluminium mast and said, 'From this angle, you can't believe we're not going to hit the wires and barbecue the whole family.'

My daughter, pretending she had been electrically shocked, gave a theatrical little shiver and a shake, spectacularly convulsed, and slid to the bottom boards. As I was laughing and pulling her up, I glanced to the masthead and gasped as I saw the windvane begin to bend at an angle, break free and come cluttering to the deck.

By some sort of miracle, we survived. Although certainly getting a great shock, it was not from the electricity. I could not believe that we had not all been vapourised. I made for the shore and a phone box to immediately call the power company to warn them of this dire situation and thus save any other masted sailing boats coming along after us.

They didn't seem fussed at all, 'Oh really, they said airily, they sometimes sag surprisingly low when we are having a run of very hot days. Nothing we can do about it for a few weeks.'

Bloody hell!

I was not happy. I sent the electricity company a bill for my windvane, and a new pair of underpants.

The Witching Hours

It is a dark and a stormy night, two stupid men are four miles off the coast and punching through heavy seas and blasting rain. It is two AM. Smarter sailors are in a secure anchorage and safely tucked up in their dry beds.

My mate is doing alright. He has wedged himself into a mass of sails bags in a sodden corner of the fo'c'sle and snoring slightly louder than the force seven outside.

I am mentally praising myself for my wise choice of a centre cockpit ketch with an enclosed pilot house. No rain cascading off the main and running down my neck and dribbling into my knickers for me. Been there, done that. On my good ship *Miranda*, I am nice and dry, the stereo is playing gently, and I glance occasionally at the rain washed-out radar and peer through the rain splashed windows in search of any other vessel's lights. There's nobody else out here, but oh, what a good boy am I. Still, can't really see from inside here so probably best to pop the old head out into the open cockpit for a proper peep around.

Donning spray jacket and waterproof trousers, I climb the three short steps to the cockpit door. I push against it. It seems to have stuck, but I manage to crack it open sufficient for a blast of rain to hit my glasses. Something heavy seems to have fallen against it. I manage to lever it open a bit more and there, just a few inches from my face is a huge eye staring at me. I fall back down the steps with the door slamming shut behind me. What or who the hell was that?

We have been at sea for two days and there are only two of us, right? Check. I go forward and yes; my mate is still asleep in the forward bunk. So, how can anybody be in my cockpit? I go back to the wheelhouse and peep again. Through the rain splashed window I can make out the outlines of a hunched figure. Could it be an alien?

Brave soul that I am, I go and wake my mate for reinforcements for the coming confrontation. He is none too pleased. He says he's not on watch for another two hours. I am blathering about someone being in the cockpit. He sniffs my breath. None too convinced of my sobriety, begrudgingly and shaking his head, he drags himself out of his warm berth and follows me up to the wheelhouse. Muttering, he stands behind me as I attempt to open the door again. It opens outwards for about an inch, but beyond that it will not budge.

Through the rain splattered cockpit window, I can see a bulky body still slumped over the door and once again it turns its ghastly eye to meet mine. Bugger this! I give the door a mighty heave and tumble half out into the cockpit. Looking slightly miffed by the shoving, the biggest creature I have seen is slumped across from me in a sitting position. It seems to have no legs, just this ghastly torso with an enormous eye and a hideously hooked nose.

What I am looking at is the biggest bird I have ever seen. Later, Google, tells me this is one of the rare Wandering Albatross family. These birds are so big they would have Sesame Street's Big Bird for hors d'oeuvre. They have a wingspan of four meters and commonly weigh in at 12 kilos. Once seen, never forgotten. Alfred Hitchcock would have signed him in a flash.

Our stowaway had obviously decided it was easier to hitch his way to windward rather than bothering to spread his jumbo-sized wings and fly.

Without blinking, it steadily regards my mate and me and daring us to come near. Its look is clearly saying, 'Come any closer and I'll bite your heads off.'

So, retreat we did. Firmly locking the door behind us. It wasn't until dawn that we dared venture into the cockpit again.

To our great relief our visitor had vanished No, we hadn't both been hallucinating. On the spot where he had been sitting was a big pile of poo. It was not mine.

Going Aground

Like death and taxes, it's inevitable. No matter how good you are, one day you will make a tiny mistake, a little mismanagement, or have a slight lapse in attention. There will be an unwelcome grating, or even a sucking sound, from under your keel. Your bow will rise, and your forward momentum come to an abrupt halt.

You my dear friend, have run aground. You have run ashore, grounded, beached, high and dry, left at the altar, on the rocks, left in the lurch, passed up, penniless, homeless, hit the bank, on the bank, or if you are from the Solent area in the South of England, you will be on the putty.

There are hundreds of euphemisms for this little navigational error, but when you do it, as surely you will, let's just hope you don't do it at the top of a spring tide. If it does happen this way, you could be there for a month: unless of course you are in the Solent where it's tidal complication freakily offers you a second high tide around ten minutes later. Hallelujah brother, we are saved.

For those of us less fortunate, the first thing we must ask ourselves is whether the tide rising or falling? Oh, what a stupid question. No need to check the tide tables: Murphy's Law says, of course, it is falling.

Now is the time to spring into prompt action. Depending upon your size of boat, you can rock, jump out and push, lean the boat over, back sails or move all that can be moved to the other side of the boat. Motorboats can cautiously try going astern, knowing that as they do so, their props are hitting god knows what. If it's not rocks, it will be sucking mud or sand through your engine cooling water system. And that's not good.

Having exhausted yourselves unsuccessfully going through all these manoeuvres, you collapse in the cockpit and now become aware of all the boaters happily closely passing by in the channel you missed. They have an infuriating superior air. Some, indeed, have the downright indecency to point and laugh. A pox on them.

Oh, how feeble basic human decency that fellow boat owners should sink to this base and foul behaviour. There is no word in the English dictionary that describes such taking of pleasure at the misfortune of others. Only the Germans have a word for it. Why only the Germans? Draw your own conclusions. But the word is schadenfreude.

My English heritage leads me to mislead and disguise the situation. The first thing I do is get a couple of towels and drape them over the name of the boat. I'm not having this radioed in for all and sundry! Next, when I am high and dry, I drop a ladder over the side, get out my long-handled scrubbing brushes, a couple of buckets and set them down by the keel where they can be clearly seen.

My fond delusion is that boats will think I have not run aground by accident but beached myself at a good spot for careening and hull maintenance.

If you get a call on the VHF, say, 'Just thought I would pull over out of the channel and rest up for the night.' Even so, the shroud of night, uncomfortable as the angle of the boat may be, comes as a blessing.

Float Like a Cork

I have always felt that if a horrific storm blows up and we have sea room, my sailing boat will be perfectly okay as long as we don't hit anything. Instead of sitting terrified in the cockpit, feverishly muttering prayers, the best thing for a wimp like me is to drop all sails, save for a storm jib, if there is one, lash the wheel, go below, seal all doors and hatches and put the stereo on full blast to drown out the storm. Add a few sniffs of the whisky bottle to settle the nerves and then just wait it out. If the keel doesn't fall off, we just bob around like a cork. I think the boat can take anything. It's me that can't.

Sailing out at sea and hearing a thunderous bump on the hull has occasioned many a skipper to seek a change of underwear. Alas, there are several things lurking between you and a watery grave. The list includes other boats, fishing vessels, ships, fishing pots, shipping containers and, believe it or not, whales.

Containers lost overboard from a freighter can be awash and thus hard to spot. Some of them float just below the surface, even for months on end. Unless your boat is thickly plated in steel, they can be an ocean nightmare.

So, why don't they make it so shipping containers falling off cargo ships sink? Good question. There's been much talk of it over the years and there is a tested and proven device that can do just that. Trouble is, it costs ten dollars. So why spend that? There are only a few nutcase yachtsmen out there.

How real are your chances of hitting one? The World Shipping Council estimates 1582 containers are lost at sea each year. Let's call that figure defensive. In recent times the container ship *Apus* lost 1900 containers in one go. Another ship, the *Rena* lost 900 containers. These are just two of many incidents, It's a big ocean, but there's no shortage of floating containers out there. Best defence is a prayer.

For some strange reason, some fishermen feel entitled to litter the coastal waterways with crab pots. Hiding in the swells, with just a seaweed encrusted buoy and no masted flags flying, they give no warning. Suddenly, you're in a whole minefield of the wretched things.

The fishermen don't want to chance someone raiding their pots. To them, that's far more important than the risk to a passing yacht getting the potline wrapped around the prop. If it does, it can foul the rudder or yank out the shaft to leave a hole in your boat. Diving overboard out in the ocean to swim below a crashing transom and cutting the gear free is a very risky job. The practice of laying unmarked crab pots should be pursued by the law. On my boat I have fitted spurs on the shaft that cuts through these lines.

If I had a bit more confidence, I would steam through one of these crab pot minefields and cut them all loose.

While on the subject of harvesting from the sea, encountering a fleet of trawlers at night scattered for miles across your path can lead to a white-knuckle moment. They follow no discernible course and suddenly change direction at whim. When contending with a fleet of sixty or more, forget the rules of the road at sea. Simple reason: aboard the trawlers, no one is keeping a look out. They are all back aft bending over their nets.

My solution is to head out to the most seaward one. Going between the fleet and the land is not a good pick as the whole fleet might start fishing close to the rocks or start heading for home.

I apply a similar principle when encountering ships. Again, it is just as likely there is no one awake on the bridge. My most important rule for watch keepers is not to forget to look behind.

A Whale of a Time

So, what else can go wrong? Getting mixed up in a big pod of whales is a hairy experience. Tourists pay big dollars to go out and watch the whales on their annual migration, but if you come across them out on the ocean on your own, there is always the worry it might not end well.

Most incidents occur when a boat hits a sleeping whale. It's a bit like hitting a container. And there are a few records of whales going into the attack. A fifty-ton, sixty-foot sperm whale is known to have attacked and sunk a boat. Which was fair enough really, as it was a whaling boat.

I don't like ending up in the middle of a big pod of whales alone. I was sailing along peacefully one day, about five miles off the coast on a beautiful calm evening, when I suddenly found myself surrounded by whales. They were blowing, leaping into the air and landing so close to my boat that I was getting wet from their splashing. They would suddenly leap out right beside me, twist in the air and splash down inches in front of the bow. It was the most spectacular display I've ever seen. But I couldn't help thinking any slight misjudgement on their part would see them landing right on top of my boat and I would end up in a sardine can.

I wondered about starting the engine as the vibrations are said to make them give you some distance. But then I didn't want to risk injuring them with my propeller. Putting on the sonar depth sounder is advised by some as they say it warns them off. But then others say it can attract. Take your pick. Even the choice of yacht bottom colour has been called into question, with many saying red antifouling attracts. I wonder who does all this checking with a colour chart.

It's pointless to worry about these things as there is not much you can do about them. Still, if you believe in chance and are the type to buy lottery tickets, you might tend to be a bit cautious.

When my daughter was very young, I sought to reassure her boating was very risk free compared with life on land. 'Did you know,' I said, 'Most accidents occur within a mile of home.'

'Really?' she asked, 'Why don't we move?'

Meeting Customs

If you're heading off overseas, you will have already boned up on customs requirements, know to see them before you go, and which little flag to fly to request quarantine. But we less intrepid sailors, happily pottering around our coastal creeks, can also fall under the ever-watchful eyes of our own customs officials.

Once, in the waters of the Australian Barrier Reef, I was buzzed three times by a very low flying airplane adorned with the Customs logo. To the delight of my young children, it skimmed our masthead with a roar and even waggled its wings at us. We all merrily waved back from our cockpit. Only after it was long gone did I realise that I should have switched my radio on so that they could talk to me and check us out.

On another occasion I was sailing along the coast when I discovered my VHF radio was no longer working. I called ahead on my HF radio for an electrician to come down to the boat in my next port of call. He said ring from a shore phone as soon as I get in and, even if it were around five in the morning, he would come down to fix it.

It was about five am when I tied up on the town quay and went ashore to find a telephone. The nearest one I could find was in a pub, and unbelievably at that hour, it was open. It turned out that the pub was the watering hole of the local fishing fleet and they would like to pop in for a drink after a hard night's fishing.

I made the call, but his wife answered and said he was out on a job and to call back in twenty-five minutes. What's a bloke going to do when he's stuck in a pub at crack of dawn? Well, of course I went and ordered a beer. After all, I had been up all night as well.

While I was at the bar, I chatted with another bloke who had just brought his sixty-foot sloop down from Thailand. Then I left to go back to the phone and called the technician again. He was home and he said he would meet me back at my boat.

As I arrived, two police cars and a customs car screeched to a halt on the quay beside my boat. Wow!

They surrounded my boat and said they needed to make a full search. I shuddered. Have you seen a thirty-four-foot boat with a family of four after six weeks of cruising? In horror and confusion, I told them that, since yesterday, I had only come less than a hundred miles and the nearest duty free was in Noumea: fifteen hundred miles away. But there was no stopping them. As the customs guy started emptying every jam-packed locker, I faced a barrage of questions.

Fortunately, the radio guy arrived, looking very puzzled at the scene in front of him. Being a small town, it was also obvious he was familiar with members of the search party. He asked what was going on and was able to verify that I had only come eighty miles and was highly unlikely to have amassed a pile of contraband. At the same time, the zeal of the search party had come to a sudden halt at the sight of a bottomless pit of used nappies piled deep into the lazarette. These were courtesy of our youngest.

It turns out that since my early arrival at the quay, I had been followed to the pub where they saw me talk to a fellow at the bar and then make a couple of phone calls. All very suspicious stuff when they had been tipped off by the Thai police that the yacht of my new early morning bar friend was full of drugs. The local law enforcement was looking to see who turned up for the delivery. Honestly, it was not me. Otherwise, I wouldn't be writing books for a living.

Later that day, on the boat of my pub mate, the police and customs unearthed the biggest drug haul in the history of the state.

A few months later we saw another drug raid being made on a boat moored nearby. We watched with great interest as the customs officers dispatched two small white dogs to sniff over everything from bow to stern.

After a couple of hours, they obviously had no success and customs went away empty handed. However, two hours later, they were back again, this time with just one, but very enormous black dog. We found this trading-up hilarious and eagerly followed the brute's progress.

It was soon making a great fuss at the foot of the mast. At first, we thought maybe he had been taken short and was considering the mast as a serviceable lamp post. But no, he had hit pay dirt. The boom came off and bags of cocaine were being pulled out from inside the mast in another record haul.

One other hazard, particularly if you are cruising the Med, or, as in my case, the top end of Australia: keep a sharp watch on your telco bill. While still well inside domestic waters I copped some horrendous charges claiming that I was on international roaming. I wasn't. However, it's possible a signal did come in from another country. Six months later, after tendering my passport and threatening to go to that great arbiter of right and wrong, the current affairs television program, I was begrudgingly given a credit in full.

Getting a Break from Customs

In my younger days, I had more than my fair share of trouble with customs officials. My initiation at the age of sixteen was returning to Britain after my first solo trip to the continent. I had noted some cultural differences, such as whisky was a fraction of the price on the continent when compared to the price in Britain. And that's where scotch whisky comes from! Anyway, I was allowed to bring back one bottle duty-free. As my dad loved whisky, I bought one for him as a present. Although it is hard to believe today, at the age of sixteen I hated the stuff.

At seven am, in a cold and draughty customs shed, the inspecting officer was not pleased with the bottle he found in my backpack. He explained that I had a one litre bottle, which was several ounces more than the British ones. He said he would have to charge me full duty on the bottle. That was a horrendous sum. I asked if we couldn't just tip some out, looking around for a bin, but there was none in sight.

The customs officer demanded I either leave the bottle or pay the full duty. No way I was giving him my dad's whisky and I had no money for the duty. I asked him to show me on the bottle the level I was allowed to bring into stingy Britain.

He pointed below the neck. I pulled the top off and poured the vile liquid down my young throat. God, how it seared and burnt! Dreadful.

Holding up the bottle, I asked, 'How's that?'

Begrudgingly he let me through, warning 'We'll be looking out for you, sunshine.'

And look out for me they did as I took a job on a cruise ship and was popping in and out of that customs shed every couple of weeks.

By this time, unlike Britain, I was getting on very well with the Portuguese customs officers in our fortnightly visits to Lisbon. I was the manager of the ship's photography unit and an onboard gift shop. As soon as we docked, a customs officer would come along to put custom seals on all our display cabinets to ensure we didn't trade while in port. But before the first seal was put on, the customs officer would buy four Sony pocket radios from us and stack them discretely in the capacious pockets of his uniform. Only then would he place the seals on the display cabinets and storage lockers.

At the time, Sony pocket radios were the bees-knees of sexy and desirable. And that sale was not it for the day. The shop was located next to a bar, so my colleagues and I would take a seat and have a quiet drink.

No sooner had the customs guy gone, than another customs officer would arrive, break the seal, buy four radios, and reseal the cabinet. This went on for a few hours, with some of the officers returning three or four times.

Eventually, this roaring business was shut down by the Lisbon Sony agent. They complained to Sony Japan that we, and our two sister ships, were selling more Sony pocket radios in Portugal than the official Sony agents.

An Embarrassing Moment

However, back in the U.K., my relationship with British customs officer remained tentative.

On a cruise just finished, I had a birthday. In the carefree casual approach to sex common aboard ships, my mates were amused by my loyalty to my fiancée back home and found my shy onboard celibacy a source of great amusement. Accordingly, for a giggle, they presented me with a big carton containing a gross of what we used to call French letters. Alright, condoms in these less euphemistic times.

I don't know if you've ever seen a gross of French letters, but I can assure you it is not something to slip into your wallet, or pop into the back pocket for a fun night out. It is big, bulky, and quite frankly, embarrassing. In fact, just as my dear friends had intended.

I dutifully took it back to my cabin, and, knowing I was having VIP shore visitors the next day, stowed it behind a pile of dirty washing at the bottom of my wardrobe.

In the morning we docked, and straight on board came my boss from London, my parents and my young and innocent intended. They crowded into my tiny cabin, albeit with a little bit of jiggling and shuffling. When everyone was settled, I shyly went ahead with my report to my boss in front of my loved ones, putting all my papers on the small cabin table and going through the business details of the trip just completed.

There came a knock on the door and squeezing into the tiny space left in my cabin came the two biggest British customs officers I have ever seen. Both were carrying big torches and long sticks with mirrors on the end. They had decided to do a full search of my cabin.

Manfully, I carried on with my voyage report, but all eyes were watching the two customs officers as they pulled out the drawers beneath my bunk and started poking torches and mirrors into every conceivable hiding place. As I struggled on with my report, my boss, mum, dad and fiancée had their eyes swivelled to the customs officers, watching their every move.

Inevitably they came to the cupboard where I had hidden the box of French letters. As they went through my hanging clothes, memory of what I had hidden came flooding back. As I watched them starting to pick through my pile of dirty washing, my cheeks burned red. Up came the carton and as it still was sealed, the leader turned to me and asked what was in it.

My heart thumped like a Gardner diesel.

I was now flushing madly and said the stupidest thing one could ever say to a customs officer.

'I wouldn't look in there if I were you,' stammered this idiot.

He gave me a pitiful look, ripped open the box and dramatically poured out all its contents onto the coffee table. Down they came, shining and glinting in their individual foil wrapping, all over my business papers and spilling over onto the floor.

There was a moment of dead silence. There was a definite frisson in the air while everyone considered the possible implications of what they saw. Now all eyes were on me.

'It was a gift,' I stumble. Nobody believed me. They were wondering what sort of person needs to carry one hundred and forty-four condoms.

A Successful Smuggling Operation

Once, I did deliberately smuggle something into England. For a bit of company. I had two pet goldfish in my cabin. They had voyaged with me from Southampton to New Zealand and back a couple of times. Not a bad swim for a couple of goldfish and we had formed a bit of a bond.

When I was transferred to another ship, I wanted to take them with me, but I wasn't too sure how I was going to get a bowl of goldfish past customs in England. Surely, they had a couple of laws forbidding that.

The two ship's nurses said they had an idea, and they would take them off for me. On arrival in Southampton, they dressed up in their full nurse's uniforms and put the goldfish bowl on a metal tray along with a pair of forceps. They then covered the bowl with a white cloth, lightly dabbed with tomato sauce.

Down the gangway they marched, side-by-side urgently and intently, straight through the customs hall. They attracted a few official glances, but no officer was game enough to stop them and see what was under that blood-stained cloth.

Getting back to sailing, even in our own coastal waters, it

seems best to have an onboard log recording when and where you have been and listing the contact with shore stations made along the way. You never know when that customs launch will come alongside you.

Sick of the Sea

No matter what size your boat, or whether it be sail or motor, you have a very high chance at some stage of becoming seasick. And when you're tired and you have your head down over the small print on a chart sliding around on a bouncing navigation table, it can get the best of us.

Some people grow out of getting seasick. Others, like me, never do. When the first *Queen Mary* was launched, she was the biggest liner ever built. In fact, when the actress Beatrice Lille boarded the ship for her first voyage, she looked around the vast Purser's Square and asked, 'What time does this place get to England?'

Even the designers thought a ship that size would never roll. Wrong. Roll she did. Like a pig! Passengers went skittling from side-to-side down the long alleyways like a bowling ball. Urgently, the company fitted handrails, so at least they would have something to cling to.

After the invention of stabilisers and their fitting in 1957, the mammoth ship settled down to be more comfortable in rough seas.

The stabilisers were found to reduce the roll by seventy-five percent and therefore were also fitted to the first *Queen Elizabeth*. But I will tell you a little secret as someone who worked on both: they still rolled. The dining room chairs were anchored by a rope into a deck bolt. The tables were fitted with edges that could be raised to stop plates sliding onto the deck. By Cunard stewards, these were called 'twidlies', but are more commonly known as fiddles. The waiters also used to dampen the tablecloth to minimise plates and glasses sliding about. And, to ease digestion, the menu was changed to more basic fare.

I've spent most of my life on the water: big ships, small ships, big boats, small boats. I've been seasick on them all. After six years on ships. I was as sick the day I got off as the day I got on.

True, like most, I settle down in a couple of days, but if the ship cruises for three or more weeks in calm seas, the minute she starts to roll again, the sweat breaks out on my brow and...ugh.

Compounding my problem, on the original *Mary*, where I was emcee for cabin class, a sort of business class in today's speak, was a directive from my cruise director not to deviate from a pre-scripted welcome aboard speech which I had to deliver to passengers in the lounge immediately after their first dinner.

I was persuasively to tell them, very seriously, straight faced, ne'er even a hint of humour or roll of eye, that the ship was far too big, far too heavy, and far too wide, for anyone to ever, ever, have been seasick aboard the *RMS Queen Mary*. My boss was some sort of psychology expert.

We would be just entering the washing machine waters of the Bay of Biscay, when with a feverish brow, a face whiter than starched cabin sheets and with microphone clutched in a white-knuckle death grip, I would deliver this nonsense. All the while, the ship would be heaving and rolling with the guests desperately hanging onto the edges of their chained down drinks tables. This type of psychology may have worked for some passengers, but it sure didn't work for me.

Not helping at all was that I had to detail the amount of food we took aboard for the four-day Atlantic crossing. For three-thousand passengers eating ten thousand meals a day, the nausea inducing list included: seventy-seven thousand pounds of fresh meat, twenty-seven thousand pounds of poultry, eleven thousand pounds of fish, fifty thousand pounds of potatoes, thirty-three thousand pounds of fresh vegetables, seventy thousand eggs, twenty-two thousand pounds of flour, eleven thousand pounds of sugar, fourteen thousand gallons of milk, two thousand pounds of cheese, one thousand boxes of assorted fruit, three thousand quarts of ice cream and three tons of butter. Oops, I've forgotten the salt and pepper. By this time, my stomach would be rumbling like an off-balance washing machine.

Then would come the drinks list: twenty thousand bottles of beer, six thousand gallons of draft beer, fifteen thousand bottles of wine, five thousand bottles of spirits, and a partridge in a pear tree. Under fair weather conditions, the thought of the drink list would brighten me considerably.

I would next ask the men to volunteer for help with the washing up: sixteen thousand pieces of knives, forks and spoons and two hundred thousand pieces of china and glass.

Then, like a sexist pig, but it was the Sixties, I would ask for lady volunteers to help with the laundry: thirty thousand sheets and thirty-one thousand pillowcases. And don't forget the six miles of carpeting to vacuum. But there were never any volunteers: just like home really.

Two Stabilisers Please

One passenger, feeling unwell and obviously missing the welcome aboard talk, took to her cabin. She asked her stewardess if it could be seasickness?

Toeing the company line, the stewardess said, 'Don't worry madam, this ship has stabilisers.'

The lady asked for two stabilisers. Unfazed, the stewardess scurried off and came back with two seasickness tablets.

So yes, even on a big ship like the *Queen Mary*, we did occasionally have seasick passengers. Sailors like to say that at the first stage of sickness, you think you are going to die. A little while later, you reach the second stage: you wish you had.

There are some good things about storms at sea. Neither the storm or the sickness usually last long and, on a cruise ship, if you can make it to the dining room, you can just about sit anywhere you like.

Cures for seasickness? I've tried them all: tablets, injections, ginger root, acupressure wrist bands, dry biscuits, horizon staring, eye of newt, toe of frog, wool of bat and hair of dog. You name it, I've tried it. Only one I can guarantee: go sit under an oak tree.

Oddly enough, after a long time at sea and first landing back ashore, it can feel as though the earth is moving. That can make you so sick you want to get right back on your boat.

Returning to shore life takes some conditioning. At sea you are always pushing objects back on shelves away from the front edge to stop them vibrating off. It becomes a hard to break habit and you're likely to find yourself doing the same when home. This habit used to drive my mother mad.

The Nanny State

Those of us who like to go sailing and enjoy a bit of adventure are rapidly having our little avenues of pleasure closed off by the 'authorities'. Throughout the Western world, government killjoys seem to be encroaching on our personal liberties to protect us with laws and rules 'for our own good'.

Many of the restrictions being inflicted on us all are made to protect the dumbest people imaginable. To hell with those that are so downright stupid. Some might say they deserve what happens to them and at least if they die, they are bred out of the gene pool. However, they do make an important contribution to society in the form of not being too risk averse.

Even that free and easy-going mob in Australia are rapidly going from the 'she'll be right mate' state to the nanny state.

By law, we all must wear our lifejackets when crossing a bar. A terrible generalisation as, for example, if you are wearing a lifejacket in the wheelhouse of a motor cruiser and have the misfortune to get rolled by a misjudged wave, you're going to immediately float up to the deck head and have no chance of fighting the buoyancy to get out. Holding it in your hands is okay, but strapping it on?

I have also managed to row my dinghy ashore safely and successfully for the last sixty years and now suddenly I'm not safe to do it without a lifejacket. If I stuff up one day, so be it. It's my life, I should be free to decide on the risks.

Even the prime minister got done by the petty-minded bureaucrats who want to control our every living breath. This geezer had a waterside mansion with its own jetty. One day he walked down his wharf to where his dinghy was moored. His daring mission was to paddle it twenty metres to the beach.

A member of the public happened to take a photo and it was published in the newspapers. Ye gods, in a dinghy and not wearing a lifejacket! On the basis of that photograph, the wheels of authority eventually ground out the standard fine of two hundred and fifty dollars for the misdemeanour by the filthy rich prime minister. Ridiculous.

A paddle boat, on the water-starved, shallow and narrow Australian Murray River, was legally required to give the full lifeboat drill. The instructor demonstrated how to tie on the lifejacket correctly: fold your arms over the top to stop the jacket being forced up and breaking your neck and jump feet first into the water. 'Then,' he said, 'walk ashore.'

Down in Tasmania, a very successful designer and builder of large, fast passenger catamarans, was out on a handover test run of his latest model with the overseas purchaser on board.

Studying and explaining the instrumentation, the builder lost concentration and at twenty-five knots drove the huge ferry straight up on a reef. No one was hurt, but it made for interesting television and newspaper coverage. It took a fortnight for a salvage team and a spring tide to pull her off.

The embarrassments and the costs of the salvage were astronomical. But that was not enough for our big brothers in a government department located far from the sea. After a long enquiry, which occupied bureaucrats for eighteen months, the ruling came down that the builder's skipper's licence would be suspended for a year. You would have thought the huge costs and embarrassment suffered would have been punishment and lesson enough.

Circumnavigators can manage to get all the way down from Europe to New Zealand. Here authorities will board with an extremely rigorous check list of things needed before they can sail on. Rather than face all the bureaucratic regulations, many circumnavigators give Kiwi land a miss. The New Zealand excuse is that if some yacht gets into trouble, they must bear the costs of putting up planes to go look for them.

Absolute rubbish! This is nonsense about the cost of search and rescue. It's just a chance to charge the costs of operating planes or ships off to another department.

The forces should welcome an opportunity to go out and spot missing sailors. It's ideal training for the real thing of spotting enemy submarines and the illegal entry of foreign vessels.

If no yacht goes missing, what would they be doing? Would the pilots not be paid; would the planes be mothballed waiting for some action? Most likely they would be on some aerial exercises. Search and rescue is the best training exercise for them. Instead of cross-charging, they should be donating to the yacht in trouble for giving them something to practise on!

If someone wants to go adventuring, they should know the risk and not expect others to risk their own lives coming to rescue them.

Reluctantly, I concede one point. I used to wonder why driving a boat has the same breathalyser limit as propelling cars along at sixty mph hour within inches of another car doing sixty in the opposite direction. The reaction time is one pooftinth of a second and at night it is pure trust in god. That sort of split-second timing is not something boaties have to do. However, I recently moved to an area which has masses of jet skis and small boats zooming about at thirty knots in narrow channels. Suddenly the limit doesn't seem so silly.

And protective rules are everywhere. Not long ago I was at an airport bar, and spying a good bottle of red, asked for a glass. There was much consternation as the barman cast around for a corkscrew but was unable to find one. He eventually called his manager. The manager appeared, took in the scene with me sitting at the bar with tongue hanging out and explained to me that as we were inside security, the bar was no longer allowed to have a corkscrew because it was a potential weapon. Ye gods, now we're going to be screwed to death.

I was in for a long flight, so I said, charge me for three glasses and push the bloody cork in! They did.

Meet FRED

Auto helm systems are an essential aid for shorthanded, long-distance cruising. By the third day, grabbing a tiller, or spinning a wheel back and forth, for every hour of every day becomes a tad boring. So, welcome aboard a device to automatically steer a compass course for you. They are commonly called FRED: an acronym for Flipping Ridiculous Electronic Device. Well, at least I think that's what the 'f' stands for, but when the battery power suddenly fades, or for some mysterious reason the boat makes a violent ninety-degree course change, the actual terminology used has been known to vary.

Self-steering does not mean everyone gets to bed. You still need to keep watch for other boats and make position checks. This was aptly illustrated by a flybridge motor cruiser on self-steering and with both of the two crew members down below having a nap. FRED managed the theoretically impossible trick of driving a motor yacht straight through the narrow gap of a sixty-meter-deep cave in La Jolla, just north of San Diego.

The Californian Water Rescue Service was called out and lifeguards swam into the cave to save the two unfortunate sailors. Just hours after the crew had been rescued, the surf built, making it impossible to enter the cave and rescue the boat.

For several days, the imprisoned boat repeatedly smashed against the sides of the cave leaving nothing but piles of debris for the recovery crew. However, the two engines were salvaged.

San Diego Coastguard said a good rule of thumb was to

set a boat's autopilot to fall short of a harbour by at least three nautical miles out to sea. Not quite sure which button that is on my FRED, but it sounds a smart idea.

In another recent incident, a sailing boat in Queensland was on auto pilot when the solo sailor fell into the water. He spent a few hours floating naked while being inspected by sharks. Miraculously, he was spotted and plucked from the water by a passing boat. While he survived, his boat did not. It just sailed on until it finally hit a coral reef.

Lessons Learnt

- Be extra careful of falling over the side when the vessel is on auto pilot.
- Setting periodic clock and radar alarms is most advisable when sailing shorthanded.
- If you're off to cross oceans, you know it's a bit of an adventure, so don't expect rescue services to necessarily come to the rescue. You knew the risks and planned for them before you set off.
- Some decades ago, I was working on a Greek cruise ship while taking a terrible pasting from a stubborn hurricane which had no wish to move on. Off the coast of North Africa, for four days we were heaved to in seas that from the bridge could only occasionally be glimpsed through a virtual snowstorm of flying sea foam. The ship's steel plates were grinding, loosening, and leaking. The bilge pumps were not keeping up and for two days the captain was sending out mayday signals. The answers coming back from other vessels and aircraft was basically, 'What do you expect us to be able to do under these conditions?' Fortunately, the storm abated. The pumps managed to take over and get us back to port for repairs.

A TENDER BEHIND

EIGHT

Choosing a Dinghy

This can be as hard as choosing the mother ship. The humble dinghy will be an important part of your cruising life, so you must do your best to get this decision right.

Dinghies that have a lovely deep round bilge and are beautiful to row, become a bit of an eyesore when lashed upside down on the top of the coach house. They also block practically most of the view forward making cross-tacking in a busy waterway into a game of Russian roulette. Consequently, we are more inclined to go for the small ones. But when you step in, they seem determined to hurl you straight over the side. Some are so bad they would tip over on wet grass.

My wise old friend, sitting at the bar said, 'Nope, you don't want one of them buggers. What you need, my friend, is a Scottish dinghy.'

'A Scottish dinghy? I've never heard of that. What is it, some form of coracle?'

'Nope,' he says, 'It's called Scottish 'cos it don't tip.'

Thank you, Ernie.

This leads us towards a flat-bottomed fibreglass affair

with the freeboard of a water snake and is as ugly as sin.

But when cruising, you must have a tender. You need it for everything from hopping ashore, cleaning your topsides, to visiting other boats. The problem is what to do with them when you are making passage. If you can't pick it up and lash it on the foredeck, hang it on davits, or have one of those super modern boats allowing you to stow it under the cockpit, you will end up having to tow it along behind you.

Of course, you can get a little inflatable dinghy and inflate it when you get there. But they are monsters to row and skate and twirl around the surface like Torville and Dean. Besides, by the time it is lugged out from the bottom of a locker, unrolled, pumped up, oars unlashed and outboard lugged onto the transom, one can be too worn out to go ashore.

With no davits and with limited deck space, the temptation is to tow the tender. You must set the length of the tow line just right. When setting off from a marina or a mooring buoy, it should be kept very short for fear of the line wrapping itself a few times around your prop. There and then, that is the end of the day's boating.

Once underway, you need to adjust the painter length to your speed and conditions. Too long or too short and the dinghy will veer side-to-side or sink by either bow or stern.

One day, in my twenty-foot boat of the time, happily sailing along and towing a dinghy, I came within a walrus whisker of wrecking my boat on a pile of ugly rocks at the base of a towering headland.

I was cheating a bit, as I was pinching. I know I shouldn't. But I had been tacking back and forth like a sewing machine and feeling confident, or desperate enough, to try pinching around a headland on a lee shore. I think all that tacking had scrambled my brain. It's a bloody silly way of getting about.

I was still three hundred meters off, when big waves from the open sea rounded the head and swamped my dinghy and turned it turtle. My first thought was never mind: I can still make it. I would sort things out once I had cleared the head.

But the boat was no longer pointing as high. I adjust the tiller a bit, but the bow does not respond. Giving up, I push the helm right over to tack away, but nothing happens. There is no steering control whatsoever. We plough steadily on. The sunken dinghy is acting as a perfect self-steering vane and heading us straight towards the rocks.

With the helm now hard over, I pull with all my might on the painter to bring the dinghy up to my stern. But, with our forward way at five knots and the dinghy full of water, I can't budge it an inch.

I must cut the dinghy away. But, silly me, my knife is down below, and there is no time to get it. I am helpless, gripping the useless tiller with white knuckles and moments away from the rocks. The cliff face is towering above me. But it back winds us, setting the sails flapping madly. We are dead in the water and at the mercy of the waves. Then, miraculously, from the wind buffeting off the cliff, the sails fill on the other tack. I can come around and, huge sigh of relief, sail off to safety.

I never pinched up on a headland again. And now, I always keep a sharp knife handy in the cockpit.

Never Say Jump Aboard

For some years I lived on an island with thirty occupied houses and maybe about sixty weekenders. It was just a short distance from the mainland. There was a ferry service, but with the hours I worked, the only sure way of getting home late at night was to have your own dinghy. Inboard motors were still popular in small boats those days: one-cylinder affairs that went chug-chug, or pop-pop-pop. Their sounds were so individualistic you could know who was going by without looking out the window. Some of the commuters had dogs on the bow which would bark, adding another clue. Nowadays, it's a bit different. A couple of hundred houses and outboard motors, all wining away and sounding just the same.

For my commuting I was proud to be using a twelve-foot,

heavily built, old wooden boat with a small triangle of deck at the bow supporting a brass samson post. The bit of decking was useful because it gave me something to stand on when climbing up one of the wharfs on the mainland. We used to call it, 'Going to Australia.'

Of course, the advantage, or disadvantage, of living on an island is none of your mainland friends can drop in unannounced. You must invite them and give them a specific time for you to go over and pick them up.

One of my friends was a showman, always jovial and looking for amusement, whether on or off stage. I invited him over for a visit and when I approached the wharf, I spotted his merry tall and well-built figure welcoming me. He is doing a little jig while holding aloft a bottle of wine in each wide outstretched hand. A welcome visitor indeed.

As I came alongside the wharf steps, I said, 'Jump in old fellow.' Mistake. My friend did not bother with the wharf steps. He just jumped. With legs and arms wide, he landed on the plywood foredeck, went straight through and plummeted down to smash through the floorboards. I would swear he would have gone straight on to pierce the bottom of the boat but for the fortunate arrival of his crutch on top of the brass samson post. He had landed with one leg each side of the main deck beam. He winced a bit.

But all was not lost. The foredeck was wrecked but we were still floating. And he still held a bottle in each outstretched hand.

He was struggling to lift his legs out but couldn't as his feet were jammed through the floorboards. I then asked him to lift his legs as I thought I might then be able to remove his shoes and pull the floorboards off the bottom of his feet. But deck splinters ripping into his marital tackle caused a stream of profanities, some of which, even with all my years of working at sea, I had never heard before.

The only solution was to cut him out. And for that, I needed a saw. The nearest one was in my workshop at home.

Right now, a sense of calm was called for. I am always quick with ready advice: 'Stay there, old fellow,' I said. And he did: all the way back to my home.

What a sight we made: motoring across the bay with David, still with arms outstretched and a bottle of wine in each hand, impaled as a truncated figurehead on the foredeck.

Once at my house, I ignored my jetty and ran the boat straight up onto the beach. Getting my priorities right, I rescued the wine from his grasp. Then I went to get the tools to cut him free.

Beaching the Dinghy

If you run your dinghy up on the beach and want to go off and explore somewhere, you have the problem of how to secure the dinghy while you're away. You can come back and find the dinghy has been stolen and your only way of reaching the mother ship is to swim.

One person came back and found their stern bung plugs had been taken, so they stole mine. I now take my bung plugs with me, which means hopefully anyone taking my dinghy will fill-up and drown. Don't mess with me. Others take to using a length of chain to secure the boat to a nearby tree or rock.

If you have a light outboard, anything under twenty horsepower, is it a good idea to secure it with chain to a transom bolt or thwart? That way, they take the whole dinghy. Makes sense?

Happily, modern technology has come to the rescue, and now it is possible to tape a find-me gadget, such as Apple's Air Tag. in some discrete place in your dinghy This will send out a signal to your cell phone so you can track its whereabouts. That way you can not only retrieve your dinghy but exact some form of devilish retribution. I once managed to find my stolen dinghy with three kids in it. I towed them along behind me and dropped them off at a police wharf. You should have seen them run.

Women and Children First

Dinghies are sometimes thought of as a good alternative to buying a dedicated life raft. They are not. That risk was not for me and when first planning off-shore cruising, I ordered up a four-man life raft to be lashed to the deck. I even had it fitted with a special pressure switch that automatically releases the life raft. Once the canister is two or three feet below the water, the release springs open, the life raft inflates and bursts up to the surface. We hope.

At the life raft sales centre, I was given the opportunity to see inside the fibreglass canister and how the raft looked when fully inflated. I was also given an opportunity to board one floating in a swimming pool. No real trouble there, but it would definitely be a more interesting exercise in a heavy sea.

The sales guy asked if I wanted anything personal in the way of medicines to be packed inside. A personalised life raft? Wow! I had them put in an inhaler for my asthma, then thought a bit more of my other medical needs for what could be my last days. So, I added a little bottle of gin, some vermouth, and a tiny packet of olives. I might as well go out happy.

The life raft, in its sealed fibreglass container, was duly installed on my foredeck. It took two men. When they had finished, I tried to lift the canister to carry it to the side as if to throw it over the rail. I couldn't lift it. And the boat was sitting steady in the marina.

I asked how the hell in a rough sea was I meant to get it overboard. They said that come the time, my sudden extra strength would surprise me.

'Are you sure?' I asked.

'Well,' they said, 'Nobody's ever come back and complained.'

The golden rule for lifeboats is to only get in at the very last moment. The maxim is not to step down, but to step up.

Last Chance

One of the beauties of owning a ketch is that they sail themselves. But if you do go over the side, there is no chance of the boat rounding up into the wind, it will just sail on without you.

When coastal cruising on my own, I drop a long line to trail along behind. Such a line is known as 'last chance.' A towed dinghy can also serve as a last chance.

I am most likely to fall over when sailing in a light breeze on a sunny day and thus taking no care at all. Most men seem to fall over the side when leaning out to answer a call of nature. Maritime records show that many of the recovered bodies of lone sailors from the sea have their flies or zip undone. They say this proves the dangers of not going below for a call of nature. Maybe, but also possibly they just fall into the water and decide if they're going to drown, they might as well go out with a smile on their face.

Ernie Has a Story

I thought Ernie might appreciate this, so I approach the comedian in the yacht club bar to tell him the story of the open flies.

Ernie shakes his head wisely and tells the story of a preacher who fell in and his companions, unaware, sailed on without him.

He was a half-mile offshore and a jet ski happened along. He came alongside and told the preacher to hop on the back.

The preacher said: 'Thank you for the kind offer. But I have no fear. The good lord will save me.'

The jet skier shrugged and zoomed off.

Soon a sturdy launch with several people came near and one of the party excitedly spotted the preacher. They closed and reached down with their hands to pull him up.

'Thank you for the kind offer, but please, have no fear, the good lord will save me.'

Puzzled, and obviously unwanted, the launch motored on its way back to port.

A little later, a large trawler came very close. 'Heavens,' said the skipper. 'It's your lucky day. It's getting dark soon and it's a miracle we spotted you.'

They dropped a net over the side and told him to grab it and they would pull him up.

But the preacher gently said, 'Thank you, kind captain. But I have no fear as I know the good lord will save me.'

Shaking their heads, the fishermen went on their way.

Soon after, the preacher drowned. Being a preacher, and not a sailor, he rose straight to heaven, and there was his lord, just inside the pearly gates. The preacher, feeling cheated after all his years of service and loyalty, was not happy. He pointed out with great indignation. 'I have done your work all my life. And I prayed and prayed. Why did you not save me?'

Exasperated, God replied, 'Fool. I sent you a jet ski, a launch and a fishing boat. What more did you want?'

The stories of people falling in the water are legion, especially when it comes to transferring one foot from a boat into a dinghy or from shore to a dinghy. Videos of mishaps abound on YouTube. Go Google, it's good for a laugh.

Back in the yacht club bar, Ernie is just getting warmed up.

He says, 'People even get into trouble boating on the lake in London's Hyde Park. It was closing time and the hire boat manager spotted a boat still out on the lake. He picked up his megaphone and called, "Come in number 99, your time is up."

'Several minutes went by, but number 99 hadn't moved. In a hurry to get home, he pulled out his binoculars and focused on the boat. He then checked his list and realised they only had ninety boats.

'He picked up his megaphone and hailed again. "Number sixty-six, do you need help?"

Ernie is on a roll. Next, he tells me, there was this cruise ship which gets into trouble and down she goes. A married couple manage to get into a small rowboat. They are the only survivors but can see land ahead. The husband takes the oars, but the wind is strong, the night is drawing in and they are making poor progress.

The wife has an idea and starts abusing her husband for everything. He shouldn't have chosen that cruise, he is weak, he is useless, he can't manage to do anything.

A furious row erupts, and the irate husband begins to row faster and faster. The angrier he becomes, the faster he rows. His arms are spinning like a windmill in a gale and the oars are just a blur.

Soon they are running up on the beach and the wife bursts out laughing. 'I knew if I wound you up you would get us moving.'

Goin'Fishin'

I can honestly say, some of the best fun I've had in my own cruising years was not in the mother ship, but in the humble dinghy. With its shallow draft I can nose around everything from the head of shallow deserted creeks to drinking my way around an anchorage shared with a few fellow boaties.

I was never much good at fishing. All that boring hanging around holding onto a sagging line that never seems to come alive is like going to the stadium every day to watch a five-day test cricket match.

However, desperate for fresh food, I have perfected my own fishing technique. In a few moments, I can snag a big variety of fish. The catch covers everything from prawns and crabs to Barramundi and reef fish.

The trick is to be in an anchorage popular with trawler men. You must be up early in the morning when the fishermen are sorting and filleting their nights catch and the water is full of berley and both fish and seagulls are swooping and diving.

Prepare the perfect lure. It is essential to do this properly. First, take a shiny aluminium bucket and attach to the handle a length of line. The bucket must be clean and sparkly. Plastic won't do.

Next, add a layer of ice over the bottom of the bucket, not too much, about three inches is fine. Then open a slab of Australian Four X beer. You must use Four X as the can is a lovely golden yellow and we need it to catch the glint of the sun. Use about ten cans. The idea is to fill the bucket to the brim while making sure the ice can be clearly seen.

Carefully, lower the bucket into the dinghy, being sure not to tip it, and then climb down. Row over and close the bow of the trawler in the most up-wind position. Then, ship oars. By now your bucket of Four X should be showing little beads of moisture running down the sides of the cans. Angle the bucket to make sure the sun is catching it perfectly.

Let your dinghy drift into the tossed floating fish scraps. It's the only way to get the fish and we do not want to disturb any fishermen already in bed after a hard night's work. Make sure you have a fender out and silently drift along the trawler's topsides. You will probably get a bite at the first trawler, but if not, continue drifting down to the next.

You get a pull: a fisherman leans over the side and says, 'What have you got in that bucket?'

It's a bite. Up goes the line. The bucket is emptied and a few moments later dropped back down, now absolutely overflowing with a wonderful variety of seafood. The things they catch in those nets!

Lastly you row back to your mother ship, wake the crew, proudly hold up your bucket and say, 'How about that for a catch!'

And that's my little secret to successful fishing. It has never failed.

From Boat to Bar

There is a popular anchorage on the northern side of one of the Barrier Reef's islands. Although this bay is commercially developed, it has no marinas and gives off a good feeling of tropical island living while offering protection from the prevailing south-easterly wind. There are always plenty of boats in there, in fact, it is such a good place that some stay for months. It is also one of the few spots along the Australian east coast that for a good part of the year you can watch a sunset sizzling into the sea.

Due to the shallowing main beach, unless you have a catamaran, you must anchor well out in the bay. But a trip ashore in the dinghy will net you three or four restaurants, a general store, and a pub. There is always a line of dinghies along the beach outside the pub. In fact, the bay is an excellent spot from which to go dinghy cruising. There are some eight different sheltered beaches within reach by any dinghy with a small outboard.

Due to the length of stay of most boats, it becomes very much a community, with everyone knowing everyone else. So, there was some concern when one of the cruisers noticed early in the morning that old Tom's dinghy was not attached to his boat as usual. Everyone knew that old Tom's clockwork trips ashore were timed to when the bar opened.

Not only was Tom's dinghy not tied to the stern of his boat but there was also no sign of it pulled up on the beach in front of the pub. The alarm was raised, the coastguard notified, and the search began. No luck.

In mid-afternoon, a large cargo ship, moored on the other side of the island and about six miles away, prepared to up anchor to enter on the tide to a nearby port. Posting a look out on the bow to see the anchor come up clear, the deck hand was surprised to see a small rowing boat jammed between the chain and the bow. With his oars unshipped, Old Tom, was slumped on the floor of his dinghy, fast asleep.

It turned out that the previous night while he was rowing back to his boat, Tom had come over sleepy. Wind and the current had done the rest.

It is not uncommon to hear on the ship's radio requests to look out for lost dinghies with three fishermen aboard. These come mainly from commercial fishing boats into line fishing around the reefs. They send some crew off in a dory in one spot and then motor off to drop off another boat, and so on. The bloke that fishes from the bow is called Sharpie, the bloke amidships is called Guts and the poor fellow in the stern is called Bum.

When the mother boat comes to collect them, it appears they can be hard to find. It can take more than a day to find them. Not much fun being stuck out miles from the land in a tin dinghy in pursuit of career making up a meal of fish an' chips.

Watch Out for the Crocodiles

Cruising the northern waters of the Australian Great Barrier Reef is a wonderful experience, but the locals are quick to warn you of the danger of the crocodiles. They say: 'You might not see them, but they can see you.'

I am told that one of their favourite tricks is to watch where you go ashore in your dinghy and if over a couple of days, you always land in the spot, on the third time, if you beach your dinghy half in, half out of the water, they will hide underneath the stern to wait for your return. When you come back and step into the water to drag the dinghy back, they grab you by the ankles and introduce you to the death roll.

Apparently, hungry, or not, they are always on the hunt to stock up their larder. This is generally amongst the mangroves and the crocs stuff their victims between the roots for a while to soften up, ready for when they might feel in need of a quick snack.

This idea has no appeal to me and thus warned I take great care in crocodile territory. Once I returned to my dinghy in a notoriously crocodile infested spot and found the clear imprint of a crocodile pushing off into the water immediately beside my dinghy. I looked around for stones and other objects to throw and pelted the water around my inflatable, loose bottomed dinghy. Nothing stirred.

Eventually, I plucked up the courage to creep towards the dinghy, grab the end of the bow line and take off down the beach at a hundred miles an hour with my dinghy up in the air flying behind me like a kite.

It was also in this spot that I found a picnic table set up with a notice warning of the crocodiles. So, the question is, who was the picnic table for? Me or the crocodiles?

The problem is compounded by idiot tourist operators who take out groups of people in boats and entice crocs to leap out and grab the meat they are offering on long poles. Madness. It teaches crocodiles to associate snacks with boats and now, because of this stupid tactic, people are being taken from dinghies.

Further increasing the risk is that crocs are proliferating at an alarming rate due to bureaucrats, living in cities nowhere near crocodiles, declaring them a protected species. In fact, as far as crocs are concerned, it is now humans that should be the protected species

For me, dinghies and crocodiles no longer mix. Having once also had a sea snake rear up out of the water and look down on me in my low freeboard dinghy, I have now taken to putting on an outboard and going like hell straight for the shore.

Calling Unannounced

The longest and most complicated trip I made in my dinghy was a carefully planned revenge attack on an old friend. Rob had got me twice. And that could not pass without reprisal.

I confess I may have started it. Rob had a large mail order company and in one of the trade magazines I published, I had written a tongue-in-cheek poke at some of his merchandise. Rob seemed to take it in good part, and when I sailed three hundred miles up the coast to his neck of the woods, he offered to come out in his beautiful wooden motor cruiser and show me the way over a sand-bared harbour entrance that was only half-completed and thus not yet officially open. There is nothing like a bit of local knowledge and I gladly accepted as it would knock hours off my trip by an alternative channel.

We rendezvoused a mile off the bar and Rob successfully led the way. Once over, he offered to let me berth at his canal front home. 'Just follow me,' he said. 'The tide is going out and your depth sounder alarm might go off a bit, but I really know the waters around here.'

And really know the waters he did. Off we went with him leading me through the creeks to my night's anchorage. Within thirty minutes, he led me straight onto a sandbank. The tide was whistling out and all I could do was sit there, canted over at an angle the Leaning Tower of Pisa would envy. It was not a comfortable night, but we were eventually lifted on the morning tide. So, he had his revenge and fair enough. We still stayed friends.

But then came strike two. In another year on my annual migration to find the warmer waters of the north, I again met up with Rob. We rendezvoused in our respective boats at his favourite fishing spot. It was at the conjunction of a maze of mangrove channels all looking exactly the same. I found him there okay, anchored nearby, hopped into my dinghy and went aboard his boat for a very convivial lunch. Come mid-afternoon, I had to get underway again for my next destination.

With so many channels, I wasn't sure which was the best. So, he drew a mud map to show me the quickest way. 'It's a bit twisty and shallow,' he said, 'but as long as you ignore this branch channel here and this one here, and as long as you keep well over to port you will be okay.'

With the mud map in my hands, I popped back to my boat, up anchored and away. The afternoon sun was blazing down, and after a while I retreated from the cockpit into the shade of the wheelhouse.

As I motored along, I kept checking the chart. I could faintly hear his voice echoing in my head saying keep to port. I held the banks close, but then when I started to drift a bit out,

I again heard his voice say, 'A touch more to port.' This was spooky, I must have really been knocking back that wine at lunch. Then came his voice again, 'Hold that course!'

Stiffen the wombats! I was freaking out. I took a glance astern, and there in my cockpit was Rob, sitting bolt upright in my cockpit with a silly grin on his face. Was I hallucinating? No, it was Rob alright, but how the hell did he suddenly materialise in my cockpit when I had left him on his boat five miles back?

Apparently, shortly after I had left the anchorage, he jumped into his dinghy, roared after me, tied to my stern and, while I was motoring obliviously along at six knots, he had climbed up unseen into my cockpit. Now, forty-five minutes later his sudden materialisation was the stuff to give a heart attack.

When, a year later, I once found myself again in his waters, I didn't tell him I was coming. I was planning my revenge. I thought of somehow busting into his house, because that was sort of what he had done to me.

I hired a car and drove over to his place to check it out. It was at the curved end of a cul-de-sac. The house itself stood surrounded and guarded by tall walls, a pair of massive, locked gates and bristled with closed circuit TV cameras. Looking at the houses either side, it was the same story. In fact, the whole street was just rows of high walls and locked gates. Bloody rich people.

Impregnable? Not necessarily so. From previous visits, I knew the houses fronted onto the canal. And thus, my dear Watson, I deduced it was open to attack from the sea. And that was right up my alley. After all, I am a Cornishman and thus automatically, and in defence of my ancestors, wrongfully, but automatically deemed of pirate descent.

I had my ketch in a visitor marina berth at the local yacht club, about five miles away. With all the shallows and canals, there was no way I could get my forty-three feet of ketch anywhere near him. But I had my dinghy.

I did my planning. Sunday morning, he was sure to be home. I collect together a fishing line, a bucket, the Sunday newspaper, a folding chair, a big transistor radio of the ghetto blaster variety and then popped a few cans of beer into the esky. Finding his house was going to be difficult as there was five miles of twisting channels, canals and sandbanks not marked on any chart. There were hundreds of damn canals branching off everywhere and even tourist maps made it look like a mad woman's knitting. So, I invested in a local street directory book.

Rising at first light, I go for my most disreputable look. That comes easily to me: paint spattered old clothes, knees hanging out my trousers and a two-day growth on my unshaven face.

I pick up my gear and pack it into the dinghy. I heft on my little three horsepower asthmatic outboard, best suited to mix cocktails, into position and screw it to the transom. Next, I add two full jerricans of spare fuel. There and back is going to be a long trip.

About an hour later, I am there. Once in the right canal, finding which house is his is easy. His lovely old wooden motor yacht sits right out the front, secured to a stub of jetty. I quietly hide my dinghy behind her and creep up his wharf.

It is now half-six in the morning. His bedroom curtains are still closed. Softly, I take out my gear, set up my chair outside the glass doors of his bedroom, toss a fishing line into the canal, open a beer and prop my feet up on the esky. I don my biggest pair of dark sunglasses, smear a good dollop of white sun block over my nose and pull a wide-brimmed fisherman's hat down low over my ears. All set: I hunch down and open my newspaper.

Heavenly peace hangs over the scene. None of his security alarms have gone off and still no movement from the curtains. He really has a serene, beautiful spot. A waterfall is gently cascading into the far end of the pool, the patio is set with tubs of luxuriant blooms, and the water is lapping lightly at my feet.

I decide to liven things up a little. I switch on the radio, tune it to a rap station and give it full volume. I know how he hates rap.

This works. Out of the corner of my eye, I can see a little flutter in the curtains.

There is a long pause. I guess he is getting dressed. Another flutter of the curtains. Then, out he comes, not through his bedroom glass doors as I was expecting, but from somewhere behind me. This makes me a little uneasy, as although it helps with my disguise, he is a tall and muscly, powerful sort of fellow. I fear what he might do to me.

He is struggling to process the situation. I slouch down lower, looking as rough and as coarse as I can while trying to calm myself with the thought, he has always been a gentleman.

His voice is uncharacteristically high. He is incredulous. He is actually spluttering. Splendid.

'Who the hell are you?' he gasps. 'What on earth are you doing?'

I don't look up; I keep my head firmly down. 'Fishin', I grunt.

Silence, while Rob digests that one. He's taking deep breaths and seems to be struggling with some sort of deep inner conflict. 'This is private property.' He is now growling. 'You can't fish here.'

Still keeping my head down, I sniff loudly, and in my roughest voice mutter: 'Free country.'

He is casting about, trying to see how I got in here. There is a little gasp, and some more deep breathing. Astonishment, I hope. I think his heart is okay. It just seems his vocabulary is a tad limited this morning.

He raises his voice, and it is now, very firm, slow and heavy as he addresses this idiot in his private courtyard. 'You can't…come in …here …and fish.'

'Can,' says I, giving the line a little tug. 'Beer?'

No answer, but for a slight choking sound. But his shadow is now hovering close over me. Sweat begins to bead on my brow. I fear he's about to belt me into the middle of next week. I turn, rip off my hat and glasses and squeal 'Gotcha!'

After Rob has recovered, he serves me breakfast. We have now called pax. I hope.

Ramping Up Entertainment

If you have nothing better to do or are a little bored and looking for some form of diversion, go to your local boat ramp one weekend and park your car where you can watch all the action. It can be hilarious.

I have been told that during the summer of 1999, on California's Lake Isabella, some folk just starting boating, were having a problem with their brand new 22-foot Bayliner.

It wouldn't plane at all, and it was very sluggish and slow, no matter how much power was applied. After an hour of trying to make it go, they putted over to a nearby marina, thinking someone there could tell them what was wrong.

A thorough topside check revealed everything was in perfect working condition. The engine ran fine, the outdrive went up and down, the prop was the correct size and pitch. So, one of the marina guys jumped in the water to have a look underneath.

He came up choking on water as he was laughing so hard. Under the boat, still strapped securely in place, was the trailer.

Ernie is sitting in his corner of the yacht club bar. He asks me to sit for a minute while he tells me the story of Joe. He orders me a drink. So, I sit.

'Joe, tired from fishing all morning, decided to take a break, and brought the boat back to his lakefront home for a nap. Knowing he'd be going back out later; he left all his fishing equipment in the boat.

In the meantime, his wife, Jane, seeing the boat sitting idle, took the boat out to the middle of the lake and sat enjoying the sun while quietly reading her book.

After a while, a marine patrol officer comes alongside in

his motorboat and says to Jane, 'I'm sorry ma'am, but you're in a restricted fishing area.'

'But I'm not fishing,' objects Jane. 'I'm just reading a book!'

'Maybe so, but you have all the necessary equipment,' responds the marine patrol officer. 'I'm going to have to write you a ticket.'

'Fine,' snaps Jane, 'But I'll be charging you with sexual assault!'

'What?' gasps the outraged marine patrol officer. 'I haven't touched you!'

'Maybe so,' replies Jane, 'But you have all the necessary equipment.'

One last thing that puzzles me about dinghies. Why is it that we say you get on a boat, but you get in a dinghy? Sounds a bit the wrong way around to me!

Lessons Learnt

- Always have a sharp knife handy in the cockpit to cut the towline if necessary.
- You must make a choice between a dinghy that is easy to row, and easy to stow. Unfortunately, that can lead to some big decision making.
- If you go for an inflatable, for comfort it's best to have a rigid bottom. The dinghy, not you. However, this increases weight and probably means you're heading for a davit situation.
- Boats without rigid bottoms have the advantage of being able to be rolled up and stored in a voluminous locker.
- If you go for an inflatable dinghy, it is wise to invest in some assistance beyond a foot pump, to inflate the dinghy. Otherwise, your urge to go ashore will be greatly diminished.

'Come over for Coffee? We'd love to. We'll just pop the big ends back on the engine, tidy up a bit and be right with you.'

NINE

Eventually, the time must come when you need to give up some boating fun time to address the serious task of boat maintenance. And this is when you discover who your true friends are. The merest glimpse of a bit of sandpaper, and those stalwarts who've been partying under sail with you every weekend, will suddenly discover they are busy. The mere mention of scrubbing a bottom and they vaporise. You will likely be left to toil alone.

    I can't help wondering what it is about my appearance that when working on my boat in a marina, a never-ending stream of know-alls feel compelled and entitled to give their opinion of how the job I am doing should be done. Certainly, with my head down and my ass up labouring over gunwales, cockpit coamings and grab rails with either sandpaper or varnish brush in hand, I feel somewhat socially disadvantaged to engage in chat with some smart-ass sailor dressed by Harrods.

    Having the dubious advantage of fixing up brightwork since the age of eight, thank you very much, I feel I might have managed to pick up the odd clue on how to do the job.

    Even worse, is the inevitable discussion about the brand of varnish being used. I have learnt never to have a can of varnish on show. Best to decant the varnish into a plain jar, which really, we should do anyway, and then tuck the labelled can well out of sight.

But that only begs the question, whose varnish am I applying. Mention any brand and they will airily say with a superior air, 'I used to use that, but now I have switched to so and so.' Grr.

To circumvent this, I quickly reel off it has a dash of Nepalese virgin yak milk, collected on the night of a full moon, fermented in Cornish earthenware containers, with freshly squeezed eye of newt and a small dash of lemon. I am applying it with a brush made of blonde hair tips harvested from a female, lesser-spotted orangutang's left arm pit. A slightly puzzled look may cross their brows as they suspect that maybe they hadn't quite understood what I had said but are still reluctant to admit not knowing it.

So, they say, 'Really, I always use Goldspar.'

'Goldspar?' I say in surprise, forgetting the brand's leadership position and that in fact it might be what I am using, 'In my last fifty years I've never heard of that one. How do you spell it?' And they do!

They make ready to walk on, but pause to look back at my faultless brightwork, and inevitably ask 'How often do you have to do it?

'Oh, it varies. I suppose it's about twelve years since the last time.' And they walk away. If only that was true.

Another odd thing about marina know-alls: tell him there are a hundred billion stars in the galaxy and they'll believe you; tell them the varnish on your gunwale is wet and they have to touch it.

Slow Work

I used to keep an old nail polish bottle filled with varnish handy for touch-up repair jobs. That way, if someone dropped a winch handle or some heavy item on the brightwork, while the teak wound was still fresh, I would just give it a quick jab from my ever-ready nail brush bottle.

I was caught doing this one day when I stepped back to admire my touch-up handiwork with nail brush in hand. A bloke passing by on the marina, caught me, stopped, gasping at my long lengths of perfect gunwales, and said, 'Golly, she looks perfect. But it must take you a long time with that brush!'

Well, we all have our little oddities. For some years now I've been mad enough to keep my engine room painted in bright white gloss. But at least I know if there are any oil drips.

I once spent ten days devoted to doing a splendid job on all my bright work. When finished she looked magnificent. The marina I was in for this project was situated some ten miles up a river, so on the evening I finished, I decided to ride the tide head halfway back to the open sea, ready to continue on the next day. I anchored close to the riverbank and went to bed.

I awoke in the middle of the night to see the reflected light of flames flickering on the bulkhead. I leapt out of bed and raced up on deck. The bordering riverbanks were planted to the water's edge with sugar cane, and the bloody farmer had taken it into his head that tonight was the night to burn them off before harvesting. The air was thick with smoke and swirling embers stretched across the sky for miles in all directions. With no escape and red-hot embers landing all over my boat, I spent the rest of the night throwing buckets of water over my decks, cockpit and tender.

Dawn revealed my boat completely changed from her wonderful look of the previous day. There was soot everywhere and the embers had burnt numerous holes in my brand-new bright work. I was not happy.

As far as I was concerned, that was it for me and the varnish brush. When I came to repair all the damage, I stripped everything back to bare wood and recoated the easy way with Sickens wood stain. As my old dad used to say about boats, 'They all look the same at thirty paces'.

The Purchase Price is Just the Beginning

According to Bloombergs, that merciless bunch of killjoy financial analysts, the annual cost of boat maintenance is roughly ten percent of the cost of the boat. Ugh.

One of the most important aspects of boat maintenance is checking anything that can work loose before it goes rattling down into the bilges. Which reminds me of a trick a rogue racing mate once made when duelling another boat as, in frighteningly proximity, they prepared to gybe round a mark.

Both boats were in mid gybe, and only inches apart, when my mate furtively threw a handful of nuts and bolts high up into the sails of the opposing boat. As their boom swung smartly over, nuts and bolts came raining down. All the crew looked up in horror. With their attention fully diverted, my friend found sufficient advantage to edge ahead into a winning position. It was a bit of a jape, but it seems all's fair in love, war and yacht racing.

Calling in the Professionals

Inevitably, the day will come that us poor boat owners will need to call in some expert tradies to fix things up. With the complexity of some of the gear found on the average boat these days, repairs go way beyond the capabilities of the average owner.

Not that repairing plays much of a role anymore. It's more a question of diagnose and replace. Fixing a piece of gear that has malfunctioned is definitely a thing of the past. And it seems manufacturers are determined to make more money on replacement parts than on the sale of the original equipment.

I am certainly a bit of a duffer when it comes to fixing anything in the engine room. I once went on a six-week course on diesel maintenance. So, I learnt all about oil changing, topping up water, ensuring clean air flow to the engine and having clean fuel. But when at the end of the course my fellow students started asking too many questions, our instructor advised that in those situations it was best to call in a proper mechanic.

Due to their intricacy, I have never got too intimate with the entrails of my engines. Similarly, on a course covering the husband's supportive role in the birth of their baby, the lecturer picked on me to ask if I planned to be present at the birth. I confessed I did not know. After all, in all my years of driving I had never even dared look under the bonnet of my car.

But I do know every job will cost three times as much and take twice as long as the first estimate. And alas, I am one who frequently needs a tradie's help. This is in spite of knowing all the golden rules of do-it-yourself and the wisdom of not packing too many gizmos on your boat that can go wrong.

They say if it ain't broke, only a sailor will try and fix it. I subscribe more to the theory if it doesn't move and it should, spray it with WD40. If it does move and it shouldn't, strap it with gaffer tape. And, if you lose a vital part, you will find it the day after you buy the replacement.

The experts, the tradies, will come with a disarming smile and a little chuckle as they remind you that the word 'boat' is an acronym for Bring on Another Thousand. They say it's a four-letter word as all the other four-letter words were taken.

I once overheard a tradie talking to another and referring to me as the PBO. When I asked what that meant, they were hesitant and reluctant to tell me. When I pressed and said I really didn't mind, they confessed it stood for the Poor Bloody Owner.

Boat tradies have their specialities but are all expert in one thing. And that is coming up with an excuse for a delay in completing an assigned job. One of my favourites is that used by a painter who, after saying the job would take him two weeks, was now into his third.

When the owner protested, the painter said his two weeks were nautical weeks. Like a nautical mile, he explained, it is a little longer.

I like to be present on my boat while mechanical or electrical work is being done. I don't ask for quotes. I just ask them their hourly rate and say, okay, just turn up on time with all the tools you need and turn off your mobile phone. Just there, you save at least three hours.

Also, I can watch for oil being spilled into the bilges, or, my pet hate of all hates, check that sparkies are not dropping wire offcuts into the bilges. Once there, they can block the operation of a bilge pump when you need it most. Some tradies do not seem to understand that your boat is not necessarily just pottering around the bays but going out to face the real hazards of the open seas, where the mere act of standing up is equal to a high wire artist crossing the Grand Canyon.

The Glory of Yesteryear

I am standing on the wharf in Auckland city, running my eyes over an awe-inspiring barquentine: 180 feet of glory, exuding the heady tang of sailing in days of yore on the grand three-masted, square-rigged sailing ships. My longing gaze follows the maze of rigging, stretching from deck to mast heads, and the festoons of foot lines along her yards – all of these needed to carry her sixteen sails.

Colourful images burst into mind of eighteenth-century sailors swinging through the rigging, calling out 'Stand clear below' and 'Land oh.' They are singing salty shanties, heaving on the spokes of the capstan as they weigh anchor. And here comes Long John Silver, stomping across the deck on his peg leg with a colourful but foul-mouthed parrot on his shoulder. But wait it is not Long John. Reality dawns, the parrot has flown away and there in typical modern sailor's garb is the captain of this sail training ship.

He is sizing me up. Just as I am sizing up his ship. He comes across the deck to the gunwale and asks if I would like to come aboard for a look.

Would I? Indeed I would. The crew is all ashore and I guess he is alone and up for a bit of chat.

It's fascinating down below: dark, utilitarian, authentic and, although everyone is ashore, there is a hint of sweat, toil and breakfast. As we emerge once more into the sunlight, my mouth falls agape at the long sweep of his teak decks. Awe inspiring. But what is really catching my breath is the cleanliness, pure life and perfection in all that teak decking.

It is completely unsullied by the merest hint of a stain or slightly weathered patch. Nor does it show any hint of being oiled or raised ridges of grain. It is incredible. It would make a hospital operating theatre look in need of a good scrub. I have never seen such a perfect and huge area of pristine scrubbed decks.

I have been struggling and aspiring for this look on the various boats I have had for more than fifty years. From my ceaseless toiling, crawling on all fours across the deck, I have a permanent crick in my back, the hands of a navvy and calloused knees.

To get my decks sparkling like new, I have tried everything from buckets and buckets of salt water to every proprietary product ever made. For years I have haunted the shelves in my local chandlery for some new miracle product. All to only limited success. In six to twelve months, I have to do it again.

I look at the captain, 'I have never seen decks in such perfect condition. What do you use to get them this clean?'

'Holystone,' he says.

Holystone! I'm amazed. I'd only ever heard of its use in books like *Treasure Island*, but I remember it as blocks of sandstone. How did we end up using stupid chemicals when there was the forgotten magic of holystone?

I think on this and ask the captain the inevitable question, 'How often do you have to do it?'

He is ready for this, he stops, turns, and looks directly into my face. There is a hint of a grin about him and a whimsical glint in his eye. 'Every morning', he says.

Every morning! Bloody Hell. And now I know why he invited me aboard. It was for this 'gotcha' moment. Still, I guess every morning is not so bad when you have aboard some fifty hale-and-hearty young sail trainees.

So thereafter, I have stuck to my chemicals. A light sanding does wonders, but if you want your decks to last, it can only be done rarely or soon your decking will be paper thin.

And if you're wondering how holystone got its name, apparently it is attributed to being down on your knees in a prayer position and having a slab of sandstone in your hands that looks like the Holy Bible. I bet you didn't know that. Or even wanted to.

One of the worst things I see is people with a hose in one hand and a long handled scrubbing brush in the other and going hard at scrubbing teak decking in all directions. Teak can only be brushed lightly in the direction of the grain, or you will end up with ridges in the teak work and splinters in your bare feet.

However, I have finally finished my battles with both teak and varnish work. Late in life I managed to gather enough shekels together to have a boat built for me by a boat yard. That gave me the chance of specifying every detail of my new boat. I think it was one of the best times of my life.

In a discussion on the build, we came to the issue of a teak deck. 'What teak deck?' I asked. 'No teak. No teak at all.'

'But you have to have some teak. What about on the aft deck?' 'No.'

'How about on the gunwales?'

'No, no teak at all.'

'But what would we use?'

'Fibreglass for the decks and paint for the gunwales.'

They shuddered. But I have her now, and that's the way I like her. While all you suckers are toiling away with your scrubbing and varnishing, I'm off to sail the sea.

'Do you know what they call the fastest sailboat in the world?' asks Ernie.

I give him a blank stare.

He pauses for effect. 'Usain Boat.'

Lessons Learned

- Don't forget to slip your boat every twelve months to check anodes, all through hull fittings and re-antifoul.
- Ensure all your electrical systems are working.
- Check all plumbing systems are working.
- Check your fuel lines for cracking and that hose clamps show no sign of deterioration.
- Check all rubber hoses going in and out of the engine for signs of wear.
- Make sure your boat is smelling as clean as a whistle. Toilet smells are particularly objectionable. Replace both in and out water lines to the head as sea grasses can grow inside and are generally the cause of that terrible stink.
- Make sure all moving parts, such as hinges, track and zippers run easily. A can of silicone spray is your friend.
- Make sure all canvas and upholstery is properly cleaned.
- If your boat is wooden, I would need to add ten more pages to this list!

TEN

As our old Stratford mate Bill used to say, 'Good night, good night. Parting is such sweet sorrow that I'll say good night until tonight becomes tomorrow.'

Sooner or later, inevitably, the day will come when you must walk the plank and sell your boat. Oh, how fickle love can be! Hopefully, you will only be selling to buy another. Maybe you're flirting with something bigger, smaller, faster, or newer. That is allowed. After all, some people get married several times. The eye can wander. You espy some smart, sexy, new floozie, a real looker: beautiful, graceful, elegant, smooth, luscious curves and the cutest little stern you've ever seen. Of course, you've got to have her. But you have to sell your old boat first.

Then there's that period in your life when you go through upsizing until, in your late seventies, you reverse the order, and start downsizing. The general rule is that in your teens you are a dinghy sailor then, in your twenties, you buy a twenty-foot boat; in your thirties, a thirty-footer; in your forties, a forty-footer and so on. You get the idea.

Eventually, old age comes and unless you have made the money to buy a mega yacht with a crew, the order is reversed, with the boats getting smaller and smaller until you end up in a little seven-foot cherrywood number with brass handles screwed to all four corners.

If at seventy, you decide to sell your boat to buy a motor home, it just means you have lost your mind. If you come to sell your boat as you have relocated far from the sea to the centre of a large continent, remember, even in Denver, slap bang in the middle of the States and twelve-hundred miles from the sea, there is a sailing club on the local Chatfield Reservoir. So, you can keep sailing.

But whether you are bored with life and want to get out completely, or are attracted to something new, you are faced with the problem of how to get rid of the old one. Every divorcee knows that. Yes, this is a divorce, pure and simple.

Clear out all personal items and anything else you don't want to go on the boat once sold. And don't forget to check under the foreward bunk for that $1200 emergency money you stowed there. A mate I knew wept buckets of blood when he realised, he'd sold his beloved boat with a hoard of cash still intact. I guess the buyer found it and thought it a bit of a discount. Then again, it might still be there. However, if I had a pile of cash, the last place I would choose to store it would be on a boat.

Unfortunately, selling your once dream boat is often not easy. They like to say the two happiest days of your life are first, when you buy the boat and secondly, when you finally sell that boat. Both are difficult processes.

When selling, there is another very important maxim: you only get one chance to make a first impression. Your boat must present as clean, seaworthy, and smart as possible, with no extraneous just-in-case bits of junk floating around. Your buyer will want to start with a clean slate.

First you need to decide whether you want to sell the boat yourself or have a broker do it for you. There are pitfalls in both.

If you decide you want to sell her yourself, you must first rid yourself of all emotion. Not easy. And no doubt you have received numerous compliments about your boat, but all those people who used to go ooh and aah over your boat and beg if ever you want to sell, please, please, let them know, suddenly up and vanish.

Avoiding Emotional Involvement

I guess I am not emotionally suited to be a person that sells his own boat. Sure, I know more about her than any broker possibly could, but can I handle the prospective buyers? The answer is no.

I had one prospective buyer come to look at my beautiful ketch who went poking about, critically sniffing and snorting in every nook and cranny. I didn't like his comments and my blood pressure was rising. Getting impatient, I suggested he should go look at some other boats, like maybe on the Serpentine in Hyde Park.

But he ignored my insult and continued with his derisory inspection. Exasperated, I told him that was enough for one day. He looked up at me, sighed and condescendingly offered twenty per cent below the asking price.

'No way,' I growl through gritted teeth, 'It's time for you to leave.'

He then offered the full price, but by now, I was having a rush of blood. 'Get off,' I barked. 'I wouldn't sell to a peasant like you at any price.'

Not fancying a sudden swim, he hastily left the scene.

Oh, how I came to regret that. Just a little more than one year later, I finally sold the boat for thirty percent below the asking price. At home, I was not popular. But the nice couple that took her kept me in touch with my former love for many years. But could I afford that financial loss? No.

Listing Your Boat

So, for me, a broker is the way to go. They are more patient, tolerant folk, skilled in the presentation of wonderful boats to the right type of buyers rather than moronic idiots. They are the matchmakers.

Choose your broker carefully. Let's just say that while many of them are good upright traders, others will say anything to get a sale.

Be wary of your listing. Some brokers, looking for stock to sell, can stoop very low. They will call you and say they have seen your boat listed and they have a client very interested in your boat and they are certain they can sell the boat for you.

They might have one of the most advertised and promoted brokerages, but there is one word for them: charlatans. All they want is to list your boat in the hope of increasing their listings.

My last encounter with such a broker did not go well. He rang me with such a spiel and asked that although he didn't have a listing, could he please bring a sure-fire certainty to see my boat on a certain date. I went to my boat at the appointed time, and the broker, coming ten minutes late, said unfortunately his client got delayed, but please could I come back to his office and sign an authority to sell as his client was coming the next day and would be sure to buy. Like the mug I am, I signed.

Further excuse the next day was that the prospect wanted his wife to come and see the boat, but she couldn't make it until the next day. So, obligingly, the next day I went to open the boat, but withdrew to a discreet spot to see what would happen. The broker knew I was about and to satisfy my spying, a fellow, obviously not a buyer, came down and chatted to the broker for a while. When he finished, he got in his car, and drove off. By now my antennae were quivering like a cicada on heat.

I jumped in my car and followed the 'prospective buyer', right back to guess where? The sales office! There he took a seat behind his desk. I tell you this story to let you know how low some brokers can sink.

I had my revenge by emailing every marina in the area warning them of this brokerage's dishonourable tactics and suggesting they should not let any representative of this brokerage on their marinas. The response was amazing. Many said they already had suspicions of this well-known local brokerage, and that they would often call asking for a marina key to inspect a client's boat. In reality, all they were doing was walking around to spot any boats with a For Sale sign on it. They would then drop a card in the boat, or ring the number advertised and begin their spiel. Many of the marinas said they were now banning this company from their marinas. And at every talk I ever give to any yacht club, I call them out by name. Don't mess with old people.

Ernie, the yacht club comedian was at his usual place in the yacht club bar when I told him I was selling my boat. I thought he might put the word out.

Asked Ernie, 'Did you know that Vince, off *Done Racein'*, has died.

No, I didn't know that.

'Well,' he said, 'When his wife Sally went to the local newspaper office to put in an obituary notice, they asked her what she wanted to say. She shrugged and said just put 'Vince died yesterday.'

The newspaper thought that was a bit too brief and pointed out that the first five words of an obituary notice were free.

Sally thought for a moment and then said, 'Okay, put Vince died. Sailboat for sale.'

The Wake of Life

Sailors learn not only to look at the waves ahead, but those they leave behind. A watchful eye on our wake reveals our passing. Whether we are sailing too close to the wind, or making too much leeway, whether the sea is building or flattening, whether we are sober or under the influence: the waves behind us are the rippling tell-tales of our life.

But no matter how hard we strive to trim our sails, no matter how many knots we reach, no matter how hard our bow ploughs through the waves ahead, as we look back on the wake of life, we all see the same: first the waves kicking up, but slowly fading to mere ripples and finally into nothingness.

Nothing, absolutely nothing, is left to mark our passing.

So, in the meantime, remember, money can't buy happiness, but it can buy a boat.

May you have fair winds and following seas.

Selling Your Boat 171

Lessons Learned

- Remove all personal possessions and junk you have onboard
- Remove all odd tools, old cans of WD40, paint, varnish or any other maintenance object lying around.
- Strip any personal photos from bulkheads or anywhere else they have ended up.
- Send your sails off for a clean-up and repair any loose stitching and make sure no sunlight shows through. If you have three jibs and two of them look bad, just remove the two bad ones.
- Replace frayed ropes and anything that shows wear.
- Make sure the boat is properly varnished and the top sides are gleaming.
- Having the engine room professionally cleaned and repainted certainly greatly improves the look of the boat, but make sure you have the proper documentation detailing your service history. Otherwise, a prospective new buyer might think you painted to cover over something.
- Presentation is everything. Every potential buyer wants a boat that looks good. While estate agents say, location, location, location, boat buyers want looks, looks, looks.
- Open all hatches and openings and wipe around inside the rims to make sure they are sparkling clean.
- Pull together all the paperwork you have that shows

regularity of antifouling, rigging inspections and engine servicing.

- If your boat has any significant history, such as winning a race or travelling far off to some exotic island, have the documentation to prove it.
- Choosing a good time to sell is a bit of a lottery. Typically, more boats are sold at the beginning of a season than at the end, although Christmas can provide a bit of a boost. Finding the right time financially is even more difficult. The boating industry went into the doldrums for years after the 2009 financial crisis. Oddly enough, it only fully recovered with the advent of Covid in 2020. With the resulting bans on overseas travel, people not only found themselves with more money in their pockets but being out on the water with the family was one of very few escapes. The second-hand market went quickly from an over-supply to an under-supply situation.
- Before your boat is sold, start narrowing down the selection of your next boat.

TALKING THE LINGO

11

BLUNDER'S GUIDE TO THE BEAUFORT SCALE

This scale refers to constant wind speed on the open sea. According to our cover-your-ass weather forecasters gusts can be forty percent stronger. Conditions in enclosed waters will be markedly milder. But boats are meant to go to sea.

Force	Knots	Named	Sea State	Cruising Sailors' Bar Talk
0	-1	Calm	Sea surface smooth	'Haven't you got a motor on this thing?'

1	1-3	Light air	Scaly ripples no foam crests	'Might go for a row in the dinghy'
2	4-6	Light breeze	Small wavelets, crests glassy, no breaking	Flies spinnaker even though single handed.
3	7-10	Gentle breeze	Large wavelets, crests begin to break, scattered whitecap	Flies spinnaker with crew. Serves drinks.
4	11-16	Moderate breeze	Small wave 1-4 feet, many whitecaps	Perfect day. Lunch eaten underway.
5	17-21	Fresh breeze	Moderate waves 4-8 ft taking longer form, many whitecaps, some spray	Spinnaker left in locker. Lunch eaten at anchor.
6	22-27	Strong breeze	Larger waves 8-13 ft, whitecaps common, more spray	Drinks no longer served. Lunch goes over the side.
7	28-33	Near gale	Sea heaps up, waves 13-19 ft, white foam streaks off breakers	'It was blowing 55 knots and the waves were 40 feet high. Just about a hurricane'
8	34-40	Gale	Moderately high (18-25 ft) waves of greater length, edges of crests begin to break into spindrift, foam blown in streaks	'I think today, I'll go down to the boat and do a spot of maintenance.'

9	41-47	Strong Gale	High waves (23-32 ft), sea begins to roll, dense streaks of foam, spray may reduce visibility	'I can't get down to the boat this weekend.'
10	48-50	Storm	Very high waves (29-41 ft) with overhanging crests, sea white with densely blown foam, heavy rolling, lowered visibility	'Reminds me of that day we had coming back from the Isle of Wight. It was a full hurricane, we had to bail like crazy.'
11	56-63	Violent storm	Exceptionally high (37-52 ft) waves, foam patches cover sea, visibility more reduced	Road closed so couldn't make it to yacht club bar
12	64+	Hurricane	Air filled with foam, waves over 45 ft, sea completely white with driving spray, visibility greatly reduced	Recounted in the yacht club bar one week later. 'Wow, what a blow we had, we had to take in a couple of reefs.'

Dinghy Sailors' Enclosed Waters Guide to the Beaufort Scale

Force	Knots	Sea State	Dinghy Sailor
0	-1	Sea surface smooth	Discretely, let's try moving side-to-side to gently rock the boat forward.
1	1-3	Scaly ripples no foam crests	Do we have a paddle?
2	4-6	Small wavelets, crests glassy, no breaking	I think I'll bring the girlfriend.
3	7-10	Large wavelets, crests begin to break, scattered whitecap	What a great day for a sail.
4	11-16	Small waves, many whitecaps	Sailing is such fun.
5	17-21	Moderate waves taking longer to form, many whitecaps, some spray	Sailing is so exciting.

6	22-27	Larger waves with whitecaps and blinding spray	Sailing is getting too exciting. Girlfriend stays home, unless a bonzer girl who turns round and says YOU stay home!
7	28-33	Waves heap up, white foam streaks off breakers. Pray tide does not turn against wind.	If I make it home, I'm selling this boat and getting a bigger one.
8	34-40	Moderately high waves of greater length, edges of crests begin to break into spindrift, foam blown in streaks	I am never going sailing again.

Blunder's Guide to Nautical Terms (Expurgated)

Abandon Ship An imperative to leave the vessel immediately, generally signalling a rush to the yacht club bar.

Abeam A boat full of smiling sailors sitting at right angles to the vessel's keel.

Aboard On or in a vessel. Not to be confused by navigators with abroad.

Abroad A female sailing companion.

Adrift Sailing on a calm day. Sometimes used to refer to crewmen who have not returned from a pub crawl.

Aft A term used by the captain to chivvy up the crew, as in 'Stop afting about'.

Aground A call to get out and push.

Ahoy A cry to attract attention when berthing at a snooty yacht club.

Aloft Somewhere up the mast, but a no-go zone for anyone over sixty.

Amidships A position surrounded by boats.

Anchor A device for collecting mud and weed samples from the seabed.

Anchorage A popular place to drop anchor. Often identified by overcrowding and an incoming swell.

Anchor Light	Situated far from the anchor, this small light is used overnight to discharge the battery.
Anti-Fouling	A means of preventing dirty bottoms.
Ashore	On land. If unplanned, an alternative term for aground.
Avast	A large area of sail, such as a spinnaker.
Awash	Going ashore for a shower.
Backstay	A decision made by spouses in inclement weather.
Beam Sea	This is one of the four directions from which wave action causes extreme discomfort and nausea. The other directions are bow sea, quarter sea and following sea. Also caused by large motor cruisers.
Belaying Pins	Bars of iron or hard wood used to silence talkative crews.
Berth	An unexpected addition to the crew.
Bilge	The content of this glossary.
Bilge Pump	A means of ejecting incoming water to prevent a boat from sinking. Not as effective as a frightened man with a bucket.
Boat Hook	A long pole used for poking at mooring buoys and people who have fallen overboard.
Bollard	Found on quay sides and ideal for sitting on while watching boats trying to tie up.
Boom	Named after the sound made when the pole on the foot of the main sail hits someone's head.
Bow	An acknowledgment paid when the skipper shows superior boat handling skills.

Bulkhead	A dumb crew member
Calm	A Sea state often reported in the yacht club bar as force four.
Careening	A term used to excuse the fact you have run aground.
Chart	A discussion aid for locating submerged coral reefs.
Circumnavigation	A navigational error of some significance made by occasional first-time sailors.
Clew	Sometimes searched for by navigators.
Companionway	Sharing a bunk while sailing.
Course	An exercise in projected wishful thinking.
Crew	Bribed and coerced fellow sailors.
Cruising	Setting off without knowing where you are going or when you are going to get there, but a heaven-sent opportunity to do your boat maintenance away from port.
Companionway	Sharing a double bunk while sailing
Dead Reckoning	Setting a course leading to disaster.
Deck	A New Zealander term for a bit of an idiot.
Deckhead	A term used by New Zealanders for fellow crew members.
Deviation	An activity likely to attract the Sunday papers
Displacement	Coming back from ashore and being unable to find your boat.
Draught	A cold shiver when you see the distance between the bottom of the keel and the seabed.
Estimated Position	An average gained from the amalgamation of various results calculated by the crew.

Headway	Unblocking the toilet.
Heave-Ho	A result of seasickness.
Fathom	An attempt to understand why a boat has run aground.
Fender	An arm dangling over the side used to protect boat from banging into docks.
Figurehead	Very much on display but does not actually do anything.
First Mate	An imperative order to form a close union.
Fluke	An arrow-shaped heavy lump of metal. So called because if it anchors a vessel, it is a bit of a fluke.
Fore	A golfing term indicating anything forward of the mast,
Founder	The discovery of boat that broke its mooring.
Foul Wind	Created by chickens flying the coup.
Freeboard	Food and alcohol supplied by the skipper.
Gaff	A mistake made when hauling a fish aboard.
GPS	A navigator's plea to the heavens: God Preserve our Souls.
Gybe	A handy manoeuvre to rid the cockpit of unwanted crew.
Hank	An American foresail handler.
Head	Not to be confused with the poop deck, the toilet on old ships used to project from the bows, possibly to ward off other vessels. These days, it is more likely that, one way or another, the stern will be used.
Head up	Leaving the toilet seat up.

Heaving To	Two crewmen being seasick
Helmsman	A politically incorrect term for a person at the wheel.
Headway	Unjamming the toilet.
Landlubber	Someone with a nasal condition pining to get ashore.
Latitude	Required by navigator when asked for position and ETA.
LOA	Length Overall. From the foremost tip of the bow to the outermost side of a dinghy in davits. This measurement is used for bragging to your friends or offering your vessel for sale.
LOWL	Water Line Length. This shorter measurement is used for negotiating overnight berthing rates in a marina or obtaining quotes from insurance companies.
Man Overboard	The last unheard cry of someone falling overboard.
Marina	A narrow congested area for docking big boats.
Mast	A vertical pole on a vessel to support a tv antenna.
Mizzen	A mast or sail you cannot find.
Mono Hull	A half price catamaran
Motorsailer	A boat that alternates between rigging and engine problems.
Painter	A long line at the stern that used to have a dinghy on the end.
Press Gang	A group of journalists attending an America's Cup race.

Preventer	A landlubber that refuses to let her partner go sailing.
Quarter Berth	A bunk devised for contortionists.
Radar	An electronic system useful for identifying the tops of waves when it is not raining.
Reach	Brought on by seasickness. For ladies this is known as a broad reach.
Reef	The urgent command to reef'er does not mean a smoko break.
Rigging	A system of lines on sailing boats used for drying washing.
Rhumb Line	A crew lining up for a drink.
Rogue Wave	A special wave that mainly happens in bar room stories.
Rudder	The rudest person on the boat.
Race Rules	The subject of continual arguments and debates in yacht clubs.
Sailboat Race	Two or more sailing boats heading in the same direction.
Schooner	A sailboat stocked with cartons of beer and sherry.
Scuppers	An opening in the side rail to allow valuable items to run off the deck into the sea.
Sextant	A sail draped over the boom to allow discrete copulation in the cockpit.
Sea Anchor	A dropped spinnaker.
Sheet	A sheet is not a sail, but according to marine logic it is the rope attached to it.
Shroud	Used for burials at sea.
Sole	Floors, remember you have got to have soul.

Spinnaker	A large sail designed to quickly wrap several turns around the forestay. Sometimes lowered into the water to act as a sea anchor.
Splice	The joining of two ropes in holy matrimony.
Stern	Named after the look on the skipper's face when he is at the helm.
Swell	A wave that's just great.
Square Rigger	A geek rigger more than thirty years old.
Taken Aback	Upset caused by abuse hurled at a helmsman for sailing too close to the wind.
Tender	The usual condition of one's head after a night ashore
Torch	A storage device for dead batteries
V-berth	A berth that will only fit V-shaped couples.
White Horses	Generally found galloping at sea.
Yardarm	A horizontal spar which if left in a careless position will not be passed over by the sun until 11.00am and thus signalling time for the first drink of the day. For this reason, it should be hung as low as possible.
Zephyr	Rarely found but included here because it's the only thing we could find beginning with Z. It is a warm and gentle breeze much sought after by weekend sailors. It rarely occurs during weekends.

Blunder's Guide to Nautical Terms in Common Use

We have included here some examples of words used in our modern language which are derived from old nautical terms. This proves how boating is such an essential part of our way of life. No fooling around here with the definitions. So there.

Above Board Anything on or above the open deck that is in plain view and not hidden below decks.

Aloof 'Loef' is an old Dutch word which means windward. The boat that can sail closest to the wind separates from the rest of the fleet and thus stands apart.

As the Crow Flies A direct line between two points (which might cross land) which is the way crows travel rather than ships which must go around land.

At Loggerheads An iron ball attached to a long handle, used for driving caulking into seams and sometimes used in a fight. Hence: 'at loggerheads'.

At My Ropes End Sailors used the end of ropes for punishment.

Aye, Aye Reply to an order or command to indicate that it is first heard, and secondly is understood and will be carried out.

Batten Down the Hatches	Hatchways were usually covered by a grill or left open to allow fresh air circulation. However, when bad weather threatened, the crew would cover these openings with tarpaulins and fasten them in place with wooden battens.
Buttocks	Boat builders make slices of a boat lengthwise, and top to bottom. The buttock lines help to describe how the boat shape changes from centre to edge.
By and Large	By means into the wind, while large means with the wind. By and large is used to indicate a boat performs well both upwind and downwind.
Chock-a-Block	Rigging blocks that are so tight against one another that they cannot be further tightened.
Chalk it Up	At the helm, the watch keeper would record details of speed, distances, headings, etc. using chalk on a slate.
Clean Slate	At the beginning of a new watch the slate would be wiped clean.
Clean Bill of Health	A certificate issued by a port indicating that the ship carries no infectious diseases.
Clear the Deck	Removal of all unnecessary deck items in preparation for battle.
Cut Loose	To make a quick escape, a ship might cut rather than untie lashings to sails or cables for anchors, shortening the time needed get away.
Cut of his Jib	The cut of a sail refers to its shape. Since this would vary between ships, it could be used to identify a familiar vessel at a distance.

Cut and Run	Cutting away the cords on furled sails rather than untying to enable a quick departure.
Between the Devil and the Deep Blue Sea.	The devil seam is the curved seam in the deck planking closest to the side of the ship, next to the scuppers. One slip and you are swimming for your life.
Bottoms Up	Disguised members of press gangs used to trick men in pubs by giving them a beer with a shilling dropped into the bottom of their pewter tankard. Finding it when they finished their beer, they were deemed to have taken the King's Shilling and forced into joining the navy. Wising up to this trick pubs put glass bottoms into their tankards so drinkers could say 'bottoms up' and check for any hidden coins at the bottom of their glasses. Now it is an encouragement to drink or to finish one's drink
Dead in the Water	A vessel making no progress.
Deliver a Broadside	The simultaneous firing of all cannons on one side of a warship. Current common use is an attack with words.
Down in the Doldrums	The Doldrums is an area where no wind is present for weeks at a time. This means sailing vessels make little or no progress.
Devil to Pay	Paying the devil is sealing the devil seam. It is a difficult and dangerous job as it is the closest seam to the side of ship.
Dutch Courage	During the Anglo-Dutch wars in the 1600s, British propaganda claimed the Dutch troops couldn't pluck up the nerve to fight until they were fortified with copious amounts of schnapps. The term has come

	to mean false courage induced by drink.
Figurehead	Symbolic image at the head of a traditional ship to appease the sea gods. Other than that, it did nothing.
First Rate	The classification of the largest sailing warships They had three masts, 850 plus crew and more than a hundred guns.
Fits the Bill	A Bill of Lading was signed by the ship's master acknowledging receipt of specified goods for transport. Upon delivery, the goods were checked against the bill to see if all was present and correct. If so: it fits the bill.
Footloose	If the foot of a sail is not secured properly, it is footloose, blowing around in the wind.
Futtocks	On the ends of the floor timbers to extend the floor timbers; the futtocks connect the skin parts together.
Garbled	Garbling was the illegal practice of mixing cargo with garbage.
Grog	In 1770, British Admiral Vernon ordered the men's ration of rum to be watered down with an equal part of water. He was called "Old Grogram" because he often wore a grogram coat, normally made of silk and wool.
Groggy	Drunk from having consumed too much grog.
Hand over Fist	The technique of a sailor climbing shrouds on a sailing ship using hand-over-hand.
Hunky-Dory	A term invented by American sailors on R&R who used to frequent a street in Yokohama called Honcho-Dori. This street

	was known for its brothels, bars and giving sailors a good time.
Idler	Carpenters, sailmakers, cooks, etc. worked throughout the day and were thus excused from watch duty at night. They were called idlers, but not because they had nothing to do, simply because they were off duty at night. Today it refers to the inactivity of the person.
In the Offing	Anything in the water visible from land, so when a ship could be seen it was known that its arrival was imminent.
In Transit	Used in sailing as a navigation aid, especially in ports when the 'transit-line' from two 'leading lights' is used to guide vessels into port.
Junk	This was a term used for worn out ropes fit only for cutting into short lengths to make mops and mats.
Keel Over	When a boat's keel emerges from the water, the vessel is very likely to capsize
Know the Ropes	All ropes on a sailing boat have a special name to aid clear identification. Therefore, a sailor needs to know the names of all the ropes.
Landlubber	Someone who is happier on land: a land lover.
Left High and Dry	A vessel that has been grounded on a bank with no water around it due to tidal ebb or tempest.
Let the Cat out of the Bag	To break bad news. Derived from the sight of the bosun taking the cat o' nine tails out of a bag and preparing to administer a flogging.

Limey   Originally, a slang word for an English sailor due to the Royal Navy practice of issuing seamen with rations of limes to prevent scurvy.

Listless   When the wind drops and a boat is sitting upright rather than heeling from the wind, she is said to be listless and makes little headway. You know the feeling.

Long Shot   Muzzle-loading cannons were charged with more powder to propel the iron shot a greater distance. However, the more powder used the less accurate it became. So, using more powder to gain more distance greatly reduced the chance of hitting a target.

Loose cannon   In a heavy sea, a cannon could break loose from its deck fitting and start crashing from side to side causing severe injury, damage and even death.

Malingerer   Taken from the French word for sickness, sailors and soldiers who feigned sickness to avoid duty were known as a malingerer.

Tell it to the Marines Marines were soldiers carried on board to prevent a mutiny. However, the sailors thought the marines rather gullible and inclined to believe tall stories.

Nipper   Short rope used with a capstan to help raise the anchor and generally worked by the ship's boys. Hence the term for a small boy.

No Great Shakes Pieces of barrels or casks were broken down to save space. In this state they were worth very little leading to the phrase no great shakes.

No Room to Swing a Cat	All hands were assembled on deck to witness floggings. If it was very crowded the bosun might not have sufficient room to swing his cat o' nine tails.
Over A Barrel	Ship's boys were disciplined by beating their bare bottoms with a cane or cat o' nine tails while bent and tied over a gun barrel. Also known as kissing the gunner's daughter.
On the Right Tack	Taking the correct sailing course against the wind to reach a destination
Overbearing	To sail downwind directly at another ship thus blocking the wind from its sails. Another phrase used in regard to strong personalities.
Pipe Down	A signal on the bosun's pipe to signal for lights out and silence at bedtime.
Rummage Sale	A sale of damaged cargo (from French *arrimage*).
Sailing Close to the Wind	A vessel sailing unreasonably close to the wind and running the risk of being taken aback and thus pushed backwards.
Scuttlebutt	A water barrel spout for sailors who would chat while gathering around it for a drink.
Shot Across the Bows	A warning gun shot across the bows of another vessel telling it not to proceed in that direction.
Shipshape and Bristol Fashion	Bristol is an English sea port several miles from the sea. Ships that were moored there were beached at low tide. Therefore, goods in the holds needed to be securely stowed. So, a vessel mooring in Bristol would have to make sure that everything above deck

was properly secured (shipshape) as well as properly securing cargo in the hold (Bristol fashion).

Scraping the Barrel On 17th-century ships, sailors would scrape empty barrels used to store salted meat to recover remaining scraps of inferior quality.

S.H.I.T. In the 16th and 17th centuries, fertiliser was mainly distributed by sea. To save weight, it was shipped dry, but if it did get wet on the boat fermentation would start. This gives off methane and if someone lights a candle there can be a massive explosion. Although it has been disputed, bundles of manure were marked 'ship high in transit', or shit for short. You may not have heard the history of this word. I certainly hadn't. I thought it was a golfing term.

Show One's True Colours It was once common practice for ships to hoist their national flags before commencing battle. But to be able to manoeuvre into the best attack position some ships would carry flags from other countries to confuse or mislead their enemies. The true flag, or colours, might only be run up at the last moment before battle.

Skyscraper First used as a nautical term for the small, triangular sail, above the skysail. Mainly used in light winds.

Slush Greasy substance obtained by scraping the fat from empty salted meat storage barrels, or the floating fat residue after boiling the crew's meal. For collecting it, the cook could sell it for greasing parts of the running rigging.

Slush Fund	The money obtained by the cook selling slush ashore. Used for the benefit of the crew.
Son of a Gun	The space between the guns was used as a semi-private place for trysts with prostitutes and wives, which led to pregnancies. And the most convenient place to give birth was on the gun deck between the guns.
Splice the Main Brace	The mainbrace runs from the main sale main yard to the deck, much as a main sheet does on a modern sailing boat. Due to its essential role in keeping control of a vessel, attacking ships used to aim for it. If hit, the crew had to repair it as quickly as possible. In the midst of battle, this was difficult and dangerous. Afterwards, the crew would be rewarded with an extra ration of rum and thus this term for an extra drink came into being
Square Meal	When in harbour, or at sea in good weather, meals were served to the crew on a square wooden plate.
Sun Over the Yardarm	The yard is a horizontal spar used to hang square rigged sails and the yardarm is the very end of the yard. In northern latitudes the sun would appear above it at around 11.00 am.
Swinging the Lamp	Exaggerated sea stories would be exchanged at night beneath swinging lamps. Often used to indicate the storyteller is exaggerating.
Swinging the Lead	The easy job of measuring the depth of water using a lead-weighted sounding line

was often given to a sailor who was slightly sick. Feigning illness to avoid a hard job was said to be 'swinging the lead'.

Sun Over the Yardarm The yard is a horizontal spar used to hang square rigged sails and the yardarm is the very end of the yard. In northern latitudes the sun would appear above it at around 11.00 am

Take the Wind Out of his Sails A vessel moving so close to another that it steals the wind from the other vessel thus causing it to stall.

Taken Aback An inattentive helmsman sailing pointing so high he finds the wind is blowing into the sails backwards, bringing the vessel to a sudden halt.

Three sheets to the Wind This term for a drunk derives from square rigged sailing boats. A sheet is a rope line which controls the tension on the downwind side of a square sail. If, on a three masted ship, the sheets of the three lower course sails are loose, the sails will flap and flutter causing the vessel to stagger and drift aimlessly downwind.

Toe the Line When called to line up at attention, the ship's crew would form up with their toes touching a seam in the deck planking.

Touch and Go The bottom of the ship touching the bottom of the sea, but not grounding. A very risky moment averted.

Turn a Blind Eye When at the Battle of Copenhagen, a signal was given to stop fighting, Nelson held his spyglass to his blind eye and insisted he didn't see the signal. He then carried on fighting, successfully.

Turn the Corner	Pass a critical point on the way to somewhere better or safer. First used by sailors passing the Cape of Good Hope and Cape Horn
Under the Weather	Serving a watch on the weather side of the ship, exposed to wind and spray. This could lead to a sailor falling ill.
Wide Berth	Leaving room between two ships swinging on a mooring to ensure they do not touch each other.

Terra Firma

The More Firma
The Less Terror

Acknowledgements

My family of four generations, for braving boating with me.

Vincent Sapaen, for yet again invaluable help with one of my manuscripts.

Don Richardson, for his enthusiasm and encouragement with the concept for this book.

John Quirk, for his collaboration and the wonderful illustrations that bring this book to life. I heartily recommend his book *Foul Bottoms* for further reading.

Robert Tolmie, for our many weeks of boating together which helped produce content for this book.

Christopher Carrington, for his friendship and advice since we were cadet members of the Lymington Town Sailing Club. Chris went on to become a captain of super yachts and a marine surveyor, Chris helped with valuable suggestions on technical issues.

Chrissie Greening for her diligent help with the manuscript.

Peter Illidge, marine archaeologist, expert on everything on and below the waterline, for spotting my bloopers.

Dina Monks for her eagle eye on my bloopers..

Vassil Lakov for Book Design and Layout.

Ernie at the Yacht Club Bar, for stories far too corny for me to tell.

Glenfiddich Twelve-Year-Old Whisky, for inspiration.

And to you, dear kind reader, for your interest in this collection of yarns. May you have fair winds and following seas.

About the Illustrator

John Quirk

Quirky's biography would have been much shorter if the German bomb that landed outside the air raid shelter where he was being born during the blitz had gone off. After messing about in his father's boats on Midland rivers and the Bristol Channel, he headed off to East Africa where he qualified as an architect and built game lodges using unskilled labour, local materials and Swahili. He was invited to be an architect with a NY based hotel company and eight years later visited Australia and decided to stay. He has written and illustrated books ranging from making kids toys from junk to boating. He has been relating his own boating blunders as a monthly columnist for *Afloat* since 2001. and on tropical stuff ups in *Old Africa Magazine*. Sixty years on a drawing board have given his pen and watercolour drawings a distinct Quirky style.

He and his wife live on the Central coast of NSW.

John Quirk is the author of Foul Bottoms, published by Adlard Coles. John has also illustrated other books including:
How to get from January through December in Powerboating
Skipper Vs Crew and Crew Vs Skipper
The Sailor's Bluffing Bible

About the Author

Paul Curtis

Paul has sailed the South Coast of England, the Mediterranean, and the Caribbean. He has completed a circumnavigation of Australia. This took him sixty years. He did it in stages and on boats ranging from sailing yachts and motor cruisers to Cunard Queens. So, you can trust his navigational skills. He knows that to round this continent, you just need to keep Australia on the left.

In all this bumbling, Paul has gained considerable experience. He claims, at some time or other, he has made most mistakes, sometimes twice.

With a sense of humour as twisted as a spinnaker around a forestay, Paul explains cruising pitfalls and what not to do in a crisis. He loves recounting the true stories of sailors, although the use of true and sailors can be an oxymoron.

Paul's other books include
High Tea on the Cunard Queens,
Aboard Pacific Princess,
The Oasis Sisters
History of Professional Photography in Australia.

Paul likes to hear from his readers and can be contacted by email at paul@paulcurtis.com.au.
www.paulcurtis.com.au

www.ingramcontent.com/pod-product-compliance
Lightning Source LLC
Chambersburg PA
CBHW062048290426
44109CB00027B/2763